SUSAN BOYLE

LIVING THE DREAM

JOHN MCSHANE

SUSAN BOYLE

LIVING THE DREAM

THE BIOGRAPHY OF BRITAIN'S
INCREDIBLE SINGING SENSATION

JOHN BLAKE

Published by John Blake Publishing Ltd,
3 Bramber Court, 2 Bramber Road,
London W14 9PB, England

www.johnblakepublishing.co.uk

First published in paperback in 2010

ISBN: 978 1 84454 962 7

British Library Cataloguing-in-Publication Data:
A catalogue record for this book is available from the British Library.

Design by www.envydesign.co.uk

Printed in Great Britain by CPI Bookmarque, Croydon, CR0 4TD

1 3 5 7 9 10 8 6 4 2

Papers used by John Blake Publishing are natural, recyclable products
made from wood grown in sustainable forests. The manufacturing processes
conform to the environmental regulations of the country of origin.

Every attempt has been made to contact the relevant copyright-holders,
but some were unobtainable. We would be grateful if the
appropriate people could contact us.

To all who have Dreamed a Dream...

Thanks to Richard Rogers for his help in researching this book.

CONTENTS

Prologue		IX
1	DREAMING THE DREAM	1
2	THE DAY THAT CHANGED HER LIFE	15
3	A STAR IS BORN	25
4	MAKING THE HEADLINES	39
5	SUSAN GOES GLOBAL	59
6	A WEE MAKEOVER	79
7	THE PRESSURE MOUNTS	99
8	SUBO MANIA	127
9	REALITY BITES	149
10	FAME & MISFORTUNES	179
11	ON THE ROAD	205
12	LIVING THE DREAM	217
13	THE WORLD AT HER FEET	257

PROLOGUE

The middle-aged woman took a dozen steps onto the stage. Her walk was a combination of nervous hesitancy and dogged determination. At one point her left hand rested briefly on her hip as she entered the spotlight, a gesture both ultra-feminine in its delicacy yet somehow gauche and inappropriate.

She wore a lace dress in a colour best described as 'dirty gold', reminiscent in appearance, and to a certain degree shape, of the tablecloths used for afternoon tea in bygone days when front rooms were reserved for 'best'. Around her waist was a large bow of the type found on cut-price chocolate boxes in discount stores on the wrong side of town.

The woman was short, stocky and overweight, creating an image that was soon to be compared to 'a piece of pork sitting on a doily'. Her face was square and her muddy-brown hair, unkempt, untidy and seemingly unbrushed, was flecked with an overgenerous sprinkling of grey.

Her stockings were dark; her shoes were light. On her right arm she wore a cheap watch, its cumbersome face worn on the underside of the wrist, and in her right hand she clutched a large microphone, carrying it in an almost belligerent manner, as if it were a weapon that she would not hesitate to use in self-defence.

The *Concise Oxford Dictionary* defines 'frump' as a noun meaning 'old-fashioned, dowdily dressed woman.' As she came to a halt in the centre of the stage, the small figure seemed to become a walking definition of the word: a person who had the air of one who seemed not just old before her time but one who had been born middle-aged. Just by looking at her one could see a sad, working-class, ageing 'wannabe' with ideas and ambitions so above her station that they would be comical if they were not so sadly delusional. It was obvious that she had been dealt a loser's hand in life and only a mixture of pity and embarrassment prevented the 3,000-strong audience at the Scottish Exhibition and Conference Centre from laughing out loud. There was an uncomfortable atmosphere – a gleeful sense of impending disaster mixed with the voyeuristic thrill of anticipating another human being's embarrassment. Many in the theatre shifted uncomfortably in their seats and glanced sideways in a knowing manner at their friends; their only decisions would be whether to laugh out loud or silently, and whether to watch unblinkingly or through their fingers to minimise the impact. It was like standing on a stormy promenade looking out to sea where the waves were about to engulf a helpless swimmer. Too terrible to watch; too engrossing to turn away.

Around the woman's neck was a thin necklace and just below that was a label with the digits 43212 just visible. Alongside them on the tag were the words '*Britain's Got Talent*'.

In between the woman and that anticipatory audience was a desk so large it should have belonged to a James Bond villain, behind which sat three judges: two men and a woman, a triumvirate of modern-day Caesars who would signal whether the gladiators in front of them should live or die.

The man with the cropped dark hair at the end of the panel scratched the end of his nose, played absent-mindedly with his pen and looked at the fact-sheet in front of him. He was businesslike as he asked, 'All right, what's your name darling?' It was said with an air not quite of boredom but with a sense that he wanted this to be over with – and over with quickly, too. There would be, after all, no sense in prolonging the agony.

'My name is Susan Boyle,' came the answer, delivered in an unmistakably Scottish accent, sharp and clear. Her casually dressed interrogator, leaning dismissively back in his chair, was Simon Cowell. He just happened to be the most powerful man in British showbusiness, a multi-millionaire with an ever-expanding empire. His image was that of a man who didn't take kindly to fools and who could be caustically dismissive of those acts he didn't rate. No platitudes, no euphemisms – no prisoners.

Alongside him sat the actress Amanda Holden. A well-known figure on British television, her role as one of the judges of the talent show – and her frequently emotional responses to the performances and life stories of the acts she saw and heard – had elevated her to another level of fame.

And completing the trio was the Piers Morgan, a former Fleet Street editor whose meteoric newspaper career was marked by controversy and who had gone on to brilliantly reinvent himself as a television personality.

All were to play a role in the events that lay ahead, but on that day in January 2009, none of them could have predicted what was about to happen. Cowell continued the questioning in a manner which seemed to indicate that he was going to be as civilised and professional as he needed to be to get the whole business over with.

'Okay, Susan, where are you from?' he asked. 'I am from Blackburn near Bathgate, West Lothian,' she replied. So far so good. But things were going to get tricky.

'And it's a big town?' Cowell continued. Susan Boyle wasn't exactly stumped by the question, but she was in no rush to respond, perhaps understandably nervous in view of the watching thousands in the auditorium and the television cameras following her every move.

'It's a collection of ... it's a collection of ... er...' she began, and then she paused as if she didn't know the answer, struggling to get clear in her mind what the answer was, '...a collection of villages.' Then she added unnecessarily, 'I had to think there.'

Perhaps she was tired. After all, she had taken six different buses to get from her home to the theatre.

'And how old are you, Susan?' Cowell asked.

'I am 47,' came the answer.

Cowell, at the time 49 himself, rolled his eyes. A mixture of laughter and groans could be heard from the audience behind him. A cruel wolf-whistle came from somewhere in the crowd. The people watching in the theatre, and the millions who later saw Susan Boyle's audition in their homes, must have feared they were watching car-crash television.

Their impression could only have been made worse by what happened next. In the uncomfortable silence that followed the revelation of her age she suddenly interjected: 'And that's just one side of me.' She then put her left hand on her hip and gyrated like a slender teenage lap-dancer. For good measure she thrust her pelvis forwards in a gesture that, on a more conventionally attractive woman, might have been interpreted as provocative but from Susan in her dowdy clothes seemed a mixture of the comic, the grotesque and the downright enough-to-put-anyone-off-their-tea.

She finished with a vigorous nod in Cowell's direction, as if half to acknowledge his presence and half to head-butt him. Cowell did what any man would do in the circumstances: he blew his cheeks out and 'moved on.' He asked what her 'dream' was and when she said it was to be a professional singer he said, 'Why hasn't it worked out so far, Susan?'

'I have not been given the chance before, but here's hoping it will change,' she replied.

Normality, if not restored, could at least be seen on the horizon again. But it would not last for long because Cowell then asked, 'Who would you like to be as successful as?'

Susan shrugged her shoulders. 'Elaine Paige, or somebody like that,' was the answer she fired back at him. Again there was a murmur around the audience. It would be difficult to find a bigger female star of West End musicals than Elaine Paige. Her list of shows, many of which she starred in, reads like an anthology of British stage hits: *Hair*, *Jesus Christ Superstar*, *Cats*, *Chess*, *Sunset Boulevard* and, perhaps most famously, *Evita*, have guaranteed her place in any theatrical Hall of Fame. And this was who Susan Boyle wanted to be like?

Piers Morgan interjected: 'What are you going to sing tonight?' and got the response, 'I am going

to sing "I Dreamed a Dream" from *Les Misérables*.'
Cowell could be heard to mutter forebodingly 'OK.
Big song.'

Big song, indeed. Some of the many artists who have
covered the testing, ultra-dramatic number include Neil
Diamond, David Essex, Aretha Franklin, Michael Ball,
Martine McCutcheon, Ruthie Henshall and Elaine Paige
herself. Now it was Susan Boyle's turn.

She gave a sign towards the show's hosts in the
wings, Anthony McPartlin and Declan Donnelly – Ant
and Dec – that she was ready to begin.

As the opening bars of the music were played,
Morgan seemed, quite understandably, to be battling to
hold back laughter, Holden looked pensive and Cowell
intense. Three thousand people behind them prepared
for the worst.

Then Susan Boyle opened her mouth and began to
sing.

She hadn't even finished the first verse before the
cheering began. Cowell's eyebrows soared upwards in
surprise, Holden's mouth dropped downwards in shock
and Morgan was at last able to laugh, but this time from
sheer pleasure.

Two minutes twenty-five seconds after she began
singing, Susan Boyle ended her song to tumultuous
applause. It had been pandemonium throughout, a
mixture of incredulity and delight. The audience had
leapt to their feet several times, like a football crowd.

Holden and Morgan, too, stood and applauded. She could have sung only half the song and the reaction would have been the same. She had been magical from the first few notes.

The dowdy woman with the eyebrows that seemed to meet in the middle, the middle-aged spinster who had 'never been kissed' and who lived alone with her cat Pebbles was on her way to stardom. Soon she was to become 'SuBo', one of the most famous women in the world.

She would be lauded by the rich and famous and become an internet phenomenon within a few days of the broadcasting of the show in the spring. But Susan Boyle would also see the dark side of fame, the pressure and the torment it can exert on people.

She would also be the catalyst that caused many question to themselves, their prejudices, their preconceptions about what we expect from the famous in the 'Age of the Celebrity'; how we want them to look, speak, behave, live their lives. Why should we be so surprised that such talent could arrive in such an unlikely form at such an unfashionable, mature age? It wasn't to be just a case of wondering what Susan Boyle was like, but also what the judgmental reaction to her appearance and demeanour said about us.

All this and more was to follow in the mayhem that became her life as she went from mundane obscurity to worldwide fame in days.

PROLOGUE

How had all of this happened? What had her life been up until those eventful few minutes centre-stage in Glasgow? And what did the future hold for 'The Hairy Angel' who had dared to 'Dream a Dream'?

CHAPTER ONE

DREAMING
THE DREAM

When she was a little girl Susan Boyle would be asked the question all small children hear throughout their early years: 'When is your birthday?' She would reply: 'I was born on April 1st.' And before anyone could say anything she'd add, as quick as a flash, 'I'm an April Fool!'

Almost half a century later that impish sense of humour, mixed with an ability to happily be the self-imposed target of a jest, would captivate the world. That and a voice that could bring grown men and women to tears.

In the intervening years Susan Boyle suffered abuse, insults and rejection. She had, in her own famous words – whether said tongue-in-cheek or not is somehow irrelevant – 'never been kissed.' And all the time she wished she could be something else; that she could inhabit a world different from the mundane one that circumstances had deemed she was a prisoner in. In that

1

she was like millions the world over. The difference was that Susan Boyle was going to make it happen. And, whether knowingly or not, she was going to make it happen not just for herself but on behalf of those countless men and women all over the world who, every day of their lives, think to themselves, 'If only…'

Susan Magdalene Boyle was born at the small Bangour Hospital, near Broxburn, 14 miles to the west of Edinburgh. The now-closed hospital was built before the First World War and designed in the popular style of the day for asylums, its original purpose being the care of psychiatric patients. Called into action in both wars to care for the wounded, it subsequently became a general hospital for the people of the area and Susan was born there on 1 April 1961. Her mother, Bridget, was a shorthand typist before she had her children; her father, Patrick, who sang in working-men's clubs in the area, had been in the Royal Engineers during the Second World War and worked as a storeman for British Leyland in nearby Bathgate. The closure of the Leyland plant in the mid-80s hit the area – originally a cotton-manufacturing centre and then a coal producing area – hard.

Susan was to say that it was from her father that the family inherited their singing voices. Bridget and Patrick had known each other at school and been together since they were 20. Susan's was not an easy birth. Her mother Bridget was in her mid-40s and Susan suffered from a lack of oxygen that was to result in learning difficulties she had to cope with all her life. As she was to recall years later: 'When I was a baby they didn't really give me much scope. They told my parents not to expect too much of me and just to play things purely by ear because I had a slight disability. My faith got me through that. You never give up on anything really; you never give up on yourself and the people around you.'

She was the youngest of nine children in a large Catholic family: Gerard, known to all as Gerry, James, John, Kathleen, Joe, Bridie, Mary, and Patricia, who sadly died from cot death.

Home for Susan and the rest of her family was a four-bedroom council house in Blackburn, about five miles away from where she was born. So what was Blackburn, with a population of about 5,000 where she was to spend her entire life, like?

When the frenzy over Susan was at its peak in 2009, there was a rumour that she would be a contestant in a forthcoming series of *I'm a Celebrity, Get Me Out of Here!*, the television show in which a host of fairly recognisable, or almost-recognisable, celebs are left alone in the jungle to fend for themselves. In the rain and dark they have to perform a series of revolting tasks in order to earn enough food to eat. The sanitary arrangements are primitive, the living conditions Spartan at best, disgusting at worst.

The suggestion that she might be in the programme prompted the Scottish comedian Frankie Boyle to remark: 'She'll sleep in a hammock above dirt teeming with spiders and snakes. How will she be able to return to Blackburn after that kind of luxury?'

Unkind no doubt, but Blackburn, although described by Susan as a 'village' is no idyllic Brigadoon. Bridget and Patrick and their eight children lived in a cramped post-war end of terrace in Yule Terrace – the family moved there shortly before Susan was born – although there was more room as her elder siblings gradually left home.

School for Susan was St Mary's Primary and later the senior school of St Kentigern's. School days have famously been called 'the happiest days of your life' and for some they might be, but for many others they are far from joyous. True, some children enjoy their time in the classroom; others merely endure it. Susan was to recall, 'I was born with a disability and that made me a target for bullies. I was called names because of my fuzzy hair and because I struggled in class. I told the teachers but, because it was more verbal than physical, I could never prove anything. But words often hurt more than cuts and bruises and the scars are still there.

'The majority of my childhood was quite happy until I started getting bullied at school. They used to knock me about a bit and try and make me cry. There's nothing worse than another person having power over you by bullying you. I didn't think I could trust anybody and it made me a bit of a sitting target.'

She went on to say that by the time she got to

secondary school she wasn't sure who was her friend or her enemy. 'I didn't make friends very easily - I did try and speak to people, but they made fun of me. I often felt pushed aside. I was often left behind at school because of one thing or another. I was a slow learner. I'm just a wee bit slower at picking things up than other people are. So you get left behind in a system that just wants to rush on, you know? That was what I felt was happening to me... I don't think the resources were there for me back then at school.

'Teachers have more specialised training now. There was discipline for the sake of discipline back then and I would get the belt every day. "Will you shut up, Susan!" Whack!'

Even at an early age Susan had a beautiful voice and when she sang at a family wedding at the age of ten she enthralled the guests. She was a musical child and, at the age of 12, her mother placed her in the choir of her local Catholic church. She sang in musicals at school too, as well as continually singing at home, especially at New Year or family celebrations. She would stand in front of the mirror holding a hairbrush as though it were a microphone and sing along to Donny Osmond – 'Puppy Love' was her favourite – or the musical *Grease*. Later she showed a liking for the music of Andrew Lloyd Webber, especially those sung by one of the finest interpreters of his songs – Elaine Paige. Susan would sing in the shower. She'd sing anywhere.

Her favourite childhood memories to this day are of

her family. 'Special moments in my childhood include when I used to go to the Ireland with my mum and dad on holiday. I went to Ireland first of all when I was six and I visited a woman called Mrs Docherty in Dungarvan House in a place called Portrush. I always remember that place because I would always go down to the seaside, everybody would be looking for me, but I was up to my backside in sand.'

When she was 18, Susan took her one and only job, as a trainee cook in the kitchens of West Lothian College. It was a six-month contract and then it stopped. After that, she did voluntary work helping the elderly while being financially supported by her parents. She did not move out of the family home, and she did not go out on dates.

'I always sang, but it was just something I did for pleasure,' she says. 'I was needed at home most of the time anyway.' On occasions Susan went to the theatre to hear professional singers. She first heard 'I Dreamed A Dream' at a production of *Les Misérables* at the Playhouse in Edinburgh. 'It took my breath away. It was amazing.' She was singing in public, too – after a fashion. Shaky, grainy footage of several of those 'performances' was to emerge once she was a star. There would be stills from them in newspapers and magazines and they too would take their place on the internet for her growing number of admirers to watch.

In 1984 Susan appeared behind the microphone at Motherwell FC's Fir Park Social Club in a singing contest between locals and visitors from the Coventry Tam O'Shanter Club after one of the visitors dropped out. A pretty, slender Susan, sporting a typical 1980s perm, sang note-perfect versions of 'I Don't Know How To Love Him' from *Jesus Christ Superstar* and Barbra Streisand's 'The Way We Were'.

One of the audience that evening was to recall after Susan became famous: 'I can remember that she was a shy young girl but also very attractive back then – she turned a few heads when she came into the club. She was not even supposed to be singing but agreed to perform for the Tam O'Shanter team because someone had dropped out.

'Even back then, I don't think anyone expected too much from her because she was so shy, but when she began singing people took notice. I watched Susan on *Britain's Got Talent* but didn't recognise her as the girl from my video until a relation called and asked if I still had the tape. It's great Susan is finally getting some recognition. She is a great singer and it seems right that at some point she would get the credit she deserved.'

In 1995 Susan went to Braehead Shopping Centre in Glasgow to audition for *My Kind of People*, a popular ITV talent show presented by Michael Barrymore, then at the height of his fame and popularity. Susan, her hair short by now and wearing a sober coat, bravely sang 'I Don't Know How to Love Him' as Barrymore pulled faces behind her back and at one stage lay on the ground pretending to look up her skirt. He ended by throwing his arms around her and giving her a mock embrace.

'I was too nervous,' she said. 'I was shaking so much I could hardly sing. I got through it, but I never made it onto television. I just wasn't ready.'

That wasn't her only failure. She entered a local talent competition a number of times from 1997 but never won the £5,000 prize. Robert Norris, who organised the Fauldhouse Miners Welfare Club competition, said, 'Susan was a very, very shy person, but when that voice came out she was absolutely wonderful. She always came to the competition on her own – I think her brother would drop her off. Susan could sing any song from any musical, it was effortless. I remember when she performed 'Somewhere Over the Rainbow' and you could have heard a pin drop. She didn't ever win, but the talent there was of a very high standard.'

In 1999 she sang the classic sad ballad 'Cry Me A River' for a charity CD recorded by the local community to celebrate the Millennium. Only 1,000 copies of the disc were made and, a decade later, they were to become collector's items. The song remained one of her favourites and she recorded it again once she was famous.

Two years later she appeared in the West Lothian Showcase talent competition final at the Deans Community High School in Livingston. She was presented with a certificate – along with around 15 other finalists – for her troubles after performing

'What I Did For Love' from the Broadway hit musical *A Chorus Line*.

Other finalists in the event organised by the West Lothian Voluntary Arts Council included a ten-year-old trumpet player and a girl singer aged 12. The audience paid £3 each to watch. There were other appearances, and other failures.

In 2001 she appeared at Linlithgow Rose Social Club, with its 70s-style decor visually reminiscent of the hit comedy series *Phoenix Nights*. One of the audience filmed the evening, and again it turned into an internet hit when it came to light years later. Wearing a long, sequined dress she bumped into a table of drinkers as she moved towards the microphone. In front of an audience of fewer than 200 people she sang 'Whistle Down The Wind' from the musical of the same name, another Andrew Lloyd Webber song, followed by 'I Don't Know How To Love Him' from *Jesus Christ Superstar*. Standing virtually stationary she then gave her version of the Jennifer Rush ballad 'The Power Of Love', accompanied by an amateur keyboard player. Once finished she pulled a funny face and hurried off stage.

There was tragedy too around this time in her life. Susan's sister Kathleen died from an asthma attack and her father also passed away, both within a relatively short space of time, leaving Susan living alone with her mother.

Susan carried on along with the karaoke machine at local pubs and bars. On Friday nights she'd sing at the

Happy Valley Hotel, while on Sundays she'd go down the road to Moran's Turf Bar. Customers recalled how she would sit drinking lemonade and eating a packet of crisps. 'We have the karaoke here just to cheer everyone up. She'd pop in and no one really paid her much attention, and if she wasn't in the mood, she'd just walk out. She's a Blackburn bairn through and through, keeps herself to herself and she does what she wants,' said one. The day after Susan took the world by storm on *Britain's Got Talent*, she went to Moran's and, to the astonishment of the crowd that Sunday got up on the tiny stage in the corner and sang 'Somewhere Over the Rainbow'. She also got a standing ovation at church that Easter and had to sign autographs on the way in.

For several years she took singing lessons from a local voice coach, Fred O'Neil, who said, 'As a singer she always had a lovely, calm, beautiful rounded voice. It is a very good instrument.'

But there was further heartache ahead.

In 2007, her beloved mother Bridget, whom Susan had cared for devotedly in her later years, died aged 91, leaving Susan alone with just her eight-year-old cat Pebbles for company in the pebble-dashed council house.

Susan carried on with her life, collecting just under £130 a week in various benefits and spending her time watching television and reading. She was a volunteer at Our Lady of Lourdes church in Whitburn, visiting the elderly, but her mother's death cast a giant shadow. She had already considered stopping singing, and for two years after Bridget's death she did not sing at all.

Much of her shopping was done at the Mill Centre in Blackburn. She regularly went to David Stein Butchers or into the Mill Café for a snack. If she fancied going further afield she would catch the No. 8 bus into Bathgate, two miles away, and have a £5.60 fish supper – her favourite meal – at Valentes takeaway. Sometimes she would have her hair styled at Val's hairdressers. She still received some abuse as she walked around the town, with youngsters calling her 'Susie Simple' – or worse.

But all this was to change and shortly Susan Boyle, middle-aged Scots spinster, would become SuBo, a true superstar. And a large part of that transformation was due to her late mother Bridget.

'She was the one who said I should enter *Britain's Got Talent*. We used to watch it together. She thought I would win. But after she died I didn't feel like singing. I wasn't up to it. Before that I sang in church choirs and I sang karaoke in the local pubs almost every week,' she said.

Susan later described the events of that *BGT* audition day in January 2009 – three months ahead of transmission – including all the preliminaries leading up to her appearance in front of the three judges who were to decide her fate. It gives a fascinating insight into her frame of mind and her attitude to the challenge that lay ahead of her.

'I'd seen the show on television, like everyone. And I

had promised my mum just before she died that I would do something with my life. So I applied for it. Filled out the application form, went through the preliminaries, went before the panel and then was lucky enough to be picked by them, too.

'The panel asked what you'd done in the past and what kind of act you had, and if you had a stage name! I just thought, well, my own name will do, won't it? I didn't know whether I needed a stage name or not. Was it enough to just put my own name down?'

She went on to describe why she will never forget audition day, 21 January. 'A lot of people dream about being on television, about making records, about entertaining people. You chance your arm and see how far you can get. But to be honest I never thought for a minute that I would get this far.

'The audition was at the Scottish Exhibition and Conference Centre. I could see the place, but I kept on taking the wrong bus. I must have changed buses about six times to get to the place and I could see it all the time. I got there hours early and sat in the holding room watching everybody do their audition one by one. Everybody kept saying to me, "Are you sure you should be at this audition?" I saw dance groups come and go, men with spoons, dogs.'

Susan described her performance of 'I Dreamed A Dream' and her dialogue with Simon Cowell, Piers Morgan and Amanda Holden – the images that millions were later to see – but she also revealed: 'My original intention was to go on in a football strip, a Celtic strip, just to get the attention. But my family told me they'd completely disown me if I did.' Luckily, perhaps, she decided not to.

'By the time I'd finished my audition I'd missed my last bus home so one of the runners got me a taxi. I was on a real high. It was like Celtic winning the cup. I'd seen a production of *Les Misérables* in Edinburgh, at the Playhouse, and I liked the mother figure. It was after my mother died that I'd seen the show and I loved the song and what it meant. I'd sort of regressed after she'd died, if you like. It was life-changing not having her to depend on so much. I had to learn to do things for myself. This was a promise that I'd made to my mum, that I'd do something with my singing. She was the reason I pursued my singing. She was the reason I became a member of choirs and sang in wee clubs. Just to see what I could do. She had a good belief that I could do it. She was a good woman. We'd seen a soloist singing on the TV just before she passed and I said, "Is that what you want me to do, Mum?" and she said, "Yes." I said, "Are you serious?" and she said, "Of course I am."' So Susan decided to do something about it.

'My confidence was pretty down at that time. A good way of levelling it out, I found, was to tell myself that even though she's not here physically, mentally and spiritually she is. That's what keeps you going. I have my faith, which is the backbone of who I am, really.'

CHAPTER TWO

The Day that Changed her Life

Friday, 10 April 2009 was the day before the storm. The pre-recorded *Britain's Got Talent* was to be transmitted the next evening at 7.45 on ITV1 and already the newspapers were beginning to read the runes. 'Something' was about to happen. No one, however, could predict exactly what it was to be, the magnitude of what was to follow. How could they? How could anyone be prepared for the explosion that was to take place?

A smattering of small, fairly discreet, newspaper stories emerged that Friday which gave a slight but, understandably, totally underplayed hint of what was about to take place.

The sedate *Daily Telegraph* wrote: 'A 48 church volunteer who admits to having kissed is tipped to be the next winner of *Talent*. Susan Boyle, from Bathgate, astonished the judges on the ITV1 show with her rendition of 'I Dreamed A Dream' from *Les Misérables*. Simon Cowell said her voice was "extraordinary", inviting comparisons with Paul Potts, who won the show in 2007.'

The Times media correspondent wrote: 'Two years ago it was Paul Potts, the snaggle-toothed Welsh mobile phone salesman, who was propelled to international stardom by *Britain's Got Talent*, the ITV entertainment show. But the programme's producers believe that they have found an even more unlikely global singing success among this year's contestants, in the form of a reclusive 48-year-old woman from a small Scottish village, who lives alone with her cat, Pebbles. Viewers of the first episode of the show's new series, tomorrow at 7.45pm, will see Susan Boyle impress the usually caustic Simon Cowell, one of the programme's three judges, into silence. In 2007 Potts became one of the world's most unexpected singing successes after winning the show's £100,000 prize and the chance to perform for the Queen at the Royal Variety Performance.'

The Times' writer continued by telling of Susan's dialogue with Ant and Dec and then the thunderstruck reactions of the judges, noting: 'the stage is set for Ms Boyle, unemployed, from West Lothian, to follow the same path as Potts.'

Potts's album, *One Chance*, had sold more than four million copies, and it had topped the charts in 14 countries by that spring weekend in 2009. The comparison with Potts was to be continually made in the days that followed. And why not? No one could better that, could they?

Andrew Llinares, executive producer of TalkbackThames, the programme's maker, was quoted as saying: 'She was a complete revelation. Everyone was cynical about her. She's a woman who's grown up in a tiny little village and has never got married. I think the expectation was that she wasn't going to be any good. But that's what's sensational about the show. No one saw it coming.'

The Sun too recognised that there was a feeling in the air and again drew comparisons with opera-singing Potts and his rise to fame. The newspaper also wrote the first of what would turn out to be hundreds of thousands of words about Susan under the typically punchy headline: 'PAULA POTTS...Susan, a virgin at 48, is tipped to follow a Winner.'

The article began: '*Britain's Got Talent* has unearthed a female rival to opera-star winner Paul Potts – a 48-year-old Scottish VIRGIN. Susan Boyle – who admits she has "never been kissed" – is already being dubbed Paula Potts after her incredible audition. The West Lothian singleton wows judges Simon Cowell, Amanda Holden and Piers Morgan tomorrow night with her version of "I Dreamed a Dream" from the musical *Les Misérables*. She even gets a standing ovation just seconds into the song as

Simon sits there open-mouthed. But the judges are at first just as uninterested as when former Carphone Warehouse salesman Paul walked on stage back in 2007.'

The *Daily Mirror* and its Scottish-based stable-mate the *Daily Record* agreed, along with reference to her unique hairstyle. 'Jobless Scot Susan Boyle won over the *Britain's Got Talent* judges by proving herself as a surprise singing sensation,' said the Scots' newspaper, and its English counterpart noted she had the 'voice of an angel... sadly coupled with hair of a shaggy dog.' It explained to its unknowing readers that 'she has a soaring, beautiful voice that could grace a heavenly choir – but self-taught singer Susan Boyle has the hairdo from hell.'

There were, of course, other acts on the show, including a dynamic dance troupe from London called Flawless, and the *Daily Star* misread the script by giving prominence to several of the other artists ahead of Susan. The paper seemed especially interested in busty housewife Fabia Cerra, 35, a former world disco dance champion, who stripped onstage and who, at one point, lost one of her nipple tassels. The shot was censored by television chiefs for transmission – a large pair of Union Jacks were cleverly and strategically superimposed to hide her, or more likely the audience's, embarrassment.

There was little that could be done to censor 57-year-old self-styled witch Gwyneth Marichi who ended up cursing the judges, especially Simon Cowell, for their early veto of her efforts.

The *Star* noted, in a surprisingly prosaic manner: 'Other acts from the first show tipped to reach the final include father and son act Demetrios Demetriou, 40, and 14-yearold Lagi. The Greek Cypriots fool the judges into thinking they will perform a traditional Greek dance routine. But they become Stavros Flatley and strip off to show their large bellies and do their own hilarious version of Riverdance.'

It added: 'Cowell tells them: "You are one of my favourite dance acts ever." And Demetrios jokes: "I think Prince Phillip will love us."' Then, almost as an afterthought, the newspaper comments: 'Another big surprise is Susan Boyle. The drab 48-year-old from West Lothian – who claims she is single, lives with her cat Pebbles and has never been kissed – walks on stage to roars of laughter. She tells the judges she wants to be the new Elaine Paige. But within seconds she silences the giggles. She belts out "I Dreamed A Dream" from the musical *Les Misérables* and leaves everyone stunned by her amazing voice.'

Well, at least the newspaper got there in the end, although the phrase 'another big surprise' undoubtedly falls into the category of understatement of the year.

One of the oldest clichés in showbusiness – and outside of showbiz too – is the expression 'The Day That Changed My Life.' Saturday, 11 April was to be that day for Susan Boyle.

Over the breakfast tables that morning, there were more stories about Susan – still a totally unknown quantity to the nation as a whole and to the rest of the world – for the people of Britain to read. Only a tiny minority knew what she was capable of. No one knew the impact she was to have.

With showtime, albeit it pre-recorded showtime, less than 12 hours away, the momentum of the phenomenon that was to become 'SuBo' was beginning to increase, helped by the knowledge of the show that some newspapers already had. At a very slow rate, it must be said, the trickle that was to turn into a dam-bursting torrent was beginning.

Susan Boyle, the unknown, unmarried middle-aged woman from the middle of nowhere, was publicly quoted for the first time that day in a Scottish newspaper. 'I'm very proud of being 48 and never having never been kissed. It's not that I am not interested in men,' she said. 'If Mr Right comes along and it feels right then I'll get married. Mind you I'm nearly 50 so I may be left on the shelf for good soon. But it's good manners to wait until you're asked.'

The article noted that Susan had lived at home with her parents all her life and she also revealed she wanted to win the contest as a tribute to Bridget. Susan said, 'When I lost my mother I decided I wanted to do *Britain's Got Talent* for her. She was a wonderful lady – one in a million. I have four brothers and four sisters, although two have passed away, and I know they are going to back me all the way. I have been truly blessed with the family I have.'

She continued, 'At the audition I think they thought I wouldn't be good, but when I started singing the audience all got on their feet, it was fantastic. I've just been amazed by the whole thing. I've really enjoyed it so far. It's the best thing that ever happened to me.

'I'd like to go all the way. I'm doing it for Blackburn, West Lothian and the whole of Scotland.' And in a comment that looked as though it was slightly more manufactured than impromptu, she added, 'Hopefully I can show Scotland's got talent!'

Speaking to a local newspaper she also said one of the things that had driven her on was the success of a singing plumber Andrew Muir, also from West Lothian, on an earlier *Britain's Got Talent*.

'Andrew Muir was fantastic last year and somebody local going on a show like that definitely inspired me to go on. I like Elaine Paige as an artist and try to model myself on her, but it's all just for fun. I love singing. It keeps me going. It's quite an accolade what Simon Cowell said and I didn't really know what to expect. I just went and sang. It would be a dream to have a career in singing and to be on the Royal Variety Performance. I'm very pro-Royal. I'm looking forward to watching the show, although I'll probably be critical of any mistakes I see, but I'll take it all in good fun. It's only entertainment after all.'

Muir returned the compliment when he said, 'I've known Susan for quite a while and sang with her a few times at charity gigs and local talent shows in West Lothian. She's quite a character and is a really nice woman. I wish her all the best and would tell her to just go for it. There must be something in the water in West Lothian.'

The *Sun* newspaper even carried an editorial extolling her virtues: 'Susan Boyle will touch a nation's heart tonight when she sings on *Britain's Got Talent*. Her amazing voice brings the audition audience to its feet in a scene even more breathtaking than the discovery of Paul Potts. It is a feel-good story to warm the hardest of hearts.

'In these days of rampant consumerism, it is refreshing to find someone so happy with their lot. Susan has never had a boyfriend but says she couldn't have hoped for a better family life. And, as she says, you should never judge a book by its cover.'

If there was something in the West Lothian water that Andrew Muir mentioned, perhaps it would have been a good idea to bottle it and send it around the country. It is a fact worth remembering that at the time Susan was about to explode into the nation's consciousness, people in Britain really were in need of something to lift their spirits. Even Simon Cowell, a man who seemed to be on an ever-increasing spiral of success, had picked up on it.

'I truly believe this is absolutely the right time to air the show,' he explained. 'When we filmed the auditions back in January and February, things were very bad in the UK and all doom and gloom, and I did genuinely think, "Should we be doing this?" But then the reactions from the audience proved that we were right to go ahead. They were laughing and screaming and loving it. The atmosphere was great and I thought "Yes. This is exactly what we need." People need an escape and this is what I'm providing – an excuse to laugh and forget your problems.'

He added, 'If I thought Britain was broken then I wouldn't do this show. Don't write us off. I believe Britain has talent. It's feel-good, positive stuff. I know young people are often the victims of negative press. But even in the first show you'll see talented lads called Flawless who rehearse every day to be the best dancers they can be. They're not on streets causing trouble. This is what the show's about. It gives youngsters a chance to show what they can do.

'If you take all the reality talent shows there have been around the world in the past ten years, hand on heart, I think only three big international stars have emerged. They are Paul Potts from *Britain's Got Talent*, Kelly Clarkson from *American Idol* and Leona Lewis from *The X Factor*. All mine – and I am enormously proud of this fact.'

He went on to explain that the prize wasn't just performing in front of the Queen at the Royal Variety Show. 'The winner is likely to make between £250,000 and £500,000 in the first year. And who knows what will happen after that? We change people's lives.'

Throughout January and February Cowell and his co-judges sat and watched 450 acts at Manchester, Glasgow – when Susan had been one of 40 auditioning – Birmingham, London and Cardiff. In the past, winners of *BGT* and the *The X Factor* had had their lives turned around by the success the programmes had bought them, so Cowell was, of course, right when he said the show 'changed people's lives'.

But no one's life had been changed to the extent that Susan Boyle was about to experience.

Those early newspaper stories had put across the initial message that there was going to be an act with a difference on the show. But they could not even begin to illustrate the impact that the transmission of the show would shortly have.

There truly had never been anyone like Susan Boyle before…nor anything like the 'SuBo Mania' that was to come.

CHAPTER THREE
A STAR IS BORN

The millions who watched *Britain's Got Talent* that evening were in on the birth of one of – if not 'the' – most unlikely showbiz superstars of all time.

Many of them would have read in the newspapers in the preceding 48 hours about Susan, but nothing could really have prepared them for what they were to see.

To coin an old phrase, 'You had to be there'. Or its modern equivalent in the age of television, 'Did you see that?' Millions did that night – and many millions more were to watch enthralled in the weeks and months to come.

It began with a backstage shot of Susan munching on a salad sandwich and her voiceover saying, 'My name is Susan Boyle, nearly 48, currently unemployed but still looking and I'm going to sing for you on *Britain's Got Talent* today.' Then she was greeted by Ant and Dec.

Presenter Anthony McPartlin (Ant) asked 'Are you a bit nervous?' Susan replied, 'Yeah, sure I am. I am in a fighting mood you know.' She also said to the camera, 'At the moment I live alone with my cat called Pebbles. Never been married, never been kissed. Shame, but that's not an advert.' Even as she said it she pulled a face of mock self-pity and giggled. Susan, who said she had been singing since she was 12, continued, 'I've always wanted to perform in front of a large audience. I'm gonna make that audience rock.'

We have touched earlier on the reaction she received when she walked onto the stage, and on her inquisition by Simon Cowell and Piers Morgan, complete with barely-hidden looks of disbelief and apprehension on their part. Amanda Holden kept quiet, looking on in trepidation as Susan announced her choice of song, 'I Dreamed A Dream.'

And then came the song. And the cheers. And the raised eyebrows, open mouths, smiles of disbelief on the part of the panel and audience alike. Ant looked at the off-stage camera and said, 'You'se didn't expect that, did you?' Declan Donnelly winked knowingly. Morgan and Holden stood on their feet to applaud, as did the crowd.

As Susan reached the highest note of 'I Dreamed A Dream', Dec shouted 'Wow!' as Ant said 'Look at that!'

Blowing kisses to the panel and the audience she walked off to a crescendo of cheers and whistles, this time of approval rather than derision, and had to be called back by the judges to hear their verdicts.

Piers Morgan was the first to speak. 'Without a doubt that is the biggest surprise I've had in three years of this show. When you stood there with that cheeky grin and said I want to be like Elaine Paige everyone was laughing at you. No one is laughing now. That was stunning, an incredible performance. Amazing. I'm reeling from shock, I don't know about you two.'

Amanda Holden added, turning to the audience at one stage as she spoke, 'I'm thrilled because everybody was against you. I honestly think we were all being very cynical and that's the biggest wake-up call ever. And I just want to say it was a complete privilege listening to that. It was brilliant.'

Simon Cowell had a slightly different take on her performance: 'Susan,' he said, 'I knew the minute you walked out on stage that we were going to hear something extraordinary, and I was right.' Morgan and Holden laughed at his response; off-stage Dec said laughingly, 'What a load of tosh!'

Cowell continued: 'Susan, you are a little tiger aren't you?' Turning to his fellow judges, he said, 'Okay, moment of truth – yes or no?'

Piers Morgan responded with 'The biggest yes I have ever given anybody.' Holden agreed and Cowell, smilingly, said, 'Susan Boyle, you can go back to the village with your head held high, it's three yeses.'

As she left the stage, Ant and Dec took hold of her hands. Ant said, 'I think you enjoyed that just a little?' and Susan gasped, 'Didn'a half!'

Ant, as he was obliged to, then asked the obvious question – 'How do you feel?' Like a shot, the answer came back from an excited Susan: 'Bloody fantastic.'

Millions of television viewers at home had gone through the same feelings as the audience in Glasgow: the embarrassment, the sniggering, the 'Oh my God what does she look like?' moments. And they too had been stunned when Susan began to sing. The purity, the clarity, the sheer melodious pleasure that her voice gave, all were condensed into the brief time it took her to sing 'I Dreamed A Dream'. The happiness that had emanated from her, and the audience, was mirrored and then magnified by the general public. We will return later to the impact that broadcast had and the uncontrollable surge of admiration once her performance travelled across the world. It would an understatement to merely say that the effect of her performance snowballed, because this particular snowball was very shortly travelling at the speed of light. Immediately, her praises were being sung by all and sundry.

Even battle-hardened television critics were applauding.

The veteran writer and former showbiz boss Kevin O'Sullivan wrote in the *Sunday Mirror*: '"Never been married – never been kissed," reveals 48-year-old Susan Boyle, to no one's great surprise. I don't mean to be unkind... but it's safe to say that this homely Scottish spinster with striking eyebrows isn't going to win any beauty contests. And my guess is she didn't fly to Milan to buy that outfit. Cue the comedy music, cut to the audience giggling contemptuously... and prepare to laugh at another delusional loser.

'Welcome to *Britain's Got Talent* 2009 – where it looks as though the unfortunate Ms Boyle is about to experience a bucketful of ritual humiliation. But wait. Suddenly she's singing the *Les Misérables* classic 'I Dreamed a Dream'. And – oh my God – super Su has the voice of an Easter angel. Beautiful! It's a Paul Potts moment.'

The *News of the World*'s take-no-prisoners reviewer Ian Hyland said: 'No one could deny unemployed spinster Susan Boyle her moment in the sun. She may well look like the product of a drunken night involving Eddie Large and Liam Gallagher's mum but, man, can Susan belt out a show tune.'

And the *Daily Star*'s Garry Bushell echoed their views when he said: 'A wonderful show, full of fraught egos, eccentrics, bewildered amateurs and demented fools. And as well as the judges, *BGT* also delivers laughs, surprises and flashes of raw talent. Flawless, a North London dance troupe, were mesmerising. Scot Susan Boyle looked like a bag-lady dressed by Archie Mitchell, but she had a voice as sweet as a honey-bear's tooth.'

The cat was well and truly out of the West Lothian bag by now.

Soon Susan was swamped with interview requests from the British media, and gradually, piece-by-piece, her story – so ordinary on the one hand, extraordinary on the other – emerged from comments she, and those who knew her in Bathgate, were making. A comment here, a remark there, a touch of solemnity on one hand, a small joke on the other; they all formed parts of this emerging picture.

From those interviews a picture began to emerge. A picture of a woman with, to coin the modern phrase, a back-story. She was someone who was to touch millions with her struggle and the hardships she had had to bear en route to that moment of glory. Her story was to be, in a sense, mundane and uneventful. Perhaps that was one of the core reasons for the success that awaited her: there were millions out there like her who too had 'never been kissed' – never kissed by the better things in life, that is, but just hoped that one day they too would be recognised as being special in one way or another.

'I've never had a boyfriend. I've never even been kissed,' she said, repeating that infectious aside she had given Ant and Dec.

'My mother was taken ill and I was needed back at home to nurse her. My music had to take second place to that so I stopped my studies. I wanted to make her proud. I wasn't working so we scraped by on mum's pension and my benefits. It was a sad time, but I was happy at home. My parents always thought it was better I lived with them so they could keep me safe.

Looking every inch the
superstar – Susan has enjoyed
instant fame after the success
of *Britain's Got Talent*.

© *Erik Pendzich/Rex Features*

Above: A young Susan (*bottom left*) with her mother, father and family.

Below left: Susan's father, Patrick, during his time in the Royal Engineers. Patrick fought in World War Two.

Below right: Susan's mother, Bridget, with sisters Mary (*left*) and Bridie. After her mother's death, Susan felt it was time to fulfil her dream of singing professionally.

© *Photonews Scotland/Rex Features*

Susan as she first appeared on British TV – she was thrust into the
limelight after her incredible appearance on *Britain's Got Talent*.

Above left: Media frenzy heightens as paparazzi knock on Susan's door at her home in Blackburn, West Lothian.   © *Daniel Gilfeather/Rex Features*

Above right: A new look and a new confidence – Susan is snapped outside her home.   © *PA Photos*

Below: Susan became the focus of the nation's press, with reporters and photographers flocking to her house.   © *PA Photos*

Above: Practising for the big night – the final of *Britain's Got Talent*.

Below: Signing autographs for fans as the craze for SuBo grows.

© *PA Photos*

Above: Support grows as Scotland goes SuBo crazy.

Below: Fans in Susan's home town flocked to the local community
centre to watch her *Britain's Got Talent* performances.   © *PA Photos*

Shops and businesses all over West Lothian showed their support for
Susan in the run-up to the *Britain's Got Talent* final.
© *PA Photos*

Susan wows the crowds
on tour with the
Britain's Got Talent
contestants after
scooping second place
in the competition
behind dance troop
Diversity.
© *Ken McKay/Rex Features*

'My mum and dad didn't want me to have boyfriends because they were worried they would try and take advantage of me. Time went on and I just accepted it was never going to happen. It's true I've never been kissed. If someone even pecked me on the cheek it would be nice, but I've never even got that close.

'I've had crushes but never been in love. I suppose I've accepted it's never going to happen. The only thing I regret is not having children. I love kids and I would have liked to have been a mum. I've always lived at home and I still live there now. I've got the same room I had as a little girl. I am very patient,' she said. 'Circumstances can sometimes interrupt what plans you have in your life and you just have to be mature and accept that and wait for something else to come along.

'Mum loved *Britain's Got Talent* and used to tell me I should put my name down and that I'd win it if I did. But I never thought I was good enough. It was only after she died two years ago that I plucked up the courage to enter. It was a very dark time and I suffered from depression and anxiety. But out of the darkness came light. I realised I wanted to make her proud of me and the only way to do that was to take the risk and enter the show.'

And of her school days, when she was bullied, 'The teachers realised I had a voice and gave me singing parts in plays. It was the one place where I was accepted. It was a nice feeling. I still see the kids I went to school with because we all live in the same area. They're all grown up with children of their own. But look at me now. I've got the last laugh.'

She used to practise her singing all over the house. 'I love to belt out tunes in the shower because the sound is so good in the bathroom and I've got a piano in the front room to sing with. I used to have a singing teacher and piano lessons once a week, but I had to stop as I couldn't afford it.'

Susan recalled how her mother's death even made her stop singing in the church choir and the karaoke clubs and how she got back into it. 'When I heard about the auditions for *Britain's Got Talent* I decided to get back into singing and start enjoying life again. I wasn't sure how my voice would sound after so long, but the reception I got from the audience and the judges was fantastic.

'I know I'm an older woman, but I would never have had the confidence to do something like this when I was younger. I've definitely improved and got more confident as I've got older.'

She even managed to utter a remark so self-effacing it practically defies belief. 'I have been long-term unemployed and it is very difficult to find work, especially during a recession. I do voluntary work in the community to get out of the house and keep active, but hopefully this experience will help me find something. I've got bills to pay and a house to keep.

'I would like to have a career as a singer but I am just

taking small steps at the moment. I have had great support from people in the village and family, they have just told me to go for it. Obviously, I am not used to all the attention, but I am coping quite well.'

Just read that again. She had no idea what was coming.

Perhaps one of the most remarkable aspects of Susan's rise to fame is its global nature. It would be hard to find anyone so homespun, so thoroughly Scots, so ultra-ordinary British. Yet her appeal was to be universal. By 14 April – Day 3 of 'The Rest of Her Life' – she was being interviewed on ABC television news in America.

Hard on the heels of their reports on the economy and Somali pirates, the award-wining, and prestigious programme, proudly trailed their interview with Susan.

Their experienced anchorman Charles Gibson, more used to presiding over Presidential Debates, introduced her thus: 'Finally tonight, a star is born. A most unlikely star. In the world of reality TV, the young and the good looking tend to rule. So, the other night when a not especially young, and with all due respect, rather dowdy lady walked on stage for Britain's biggest TV talent show, the reaction was harsh. And then, well, hear for yourself. Here's David Muir.'

There then followed an interview between Muir, another household name to millions of Americans, and Susan. Muir intoned, 'Her name is Susan Boyle. A middle-aged church volunteer from a Scottish village.'

Footage of her being interviewed featured some of her now famous remarks.

'At the moment I live alone with my cat called Pebbles. I've never been married. Never been kissed. Shame.' This was followed by some clips of the audition overlaid with Muir's comments. 'The crowd, the judges, 11 million viewers, stunned.'

Muir finished, in that senatorial voice so essential to a newscaster in America: 'Susan Boyle, the church worker, with one God-given voice. David Muir, ABC News, New York.'

Gibson ended the report by saying, 'Her performance has been a hit online. Last time we checked the video had been watched more than 3.5 million times. More than a million just today, and she is now the overwhelming favourite to win the British talent competition.'

Ah yes, the internet, that worldwide system of interconnected computer networks that serves a global audience of billions. It has changed the world we live in and it was to change Susan Boyle's life, too.

If she had been born a generation earlier then perhaps she would not have achieved that level of fame that was to be hers. The internet, and especially the YouTube showing of her *BGT* audition, are an integral part of her story and one that we will deal with in detail later on.

That figure of 3.5 million hits on YouTube mentioned in the American newscast, phenomenal as it was in such a short space of time, would soon be dwarfed as the world logged on to Susan Boyle.

But what was it about her that generated the interest? True, her voice was wonderful, but would it have given rise to such praise if it had been coming from a singer who fitted the physical 'identikit' until then deemed necessary for stardom? Youth, glamour, a 'showbiz' personality and the flowing locks of a goddess. And sex appeal too.

None of these could be attributed to Susan. And yet, there she was, climbing to unknown heights.

But why was everyone, from the judges to that Glasgow audience, from the millions watching on television to the soon-to-be hundreds of millions on the internet, so taken aback? Why was the astonishment she generated of such proportions? Never mind what it said about Susan Boyle, what did it say about the watching world?

The Times noted: 'Susan Boyle, the dowdy Scottish spinster who dumbfounded the judges and won over the audience of *Britain's Got Talent* with her extraordinary singing voice despite, as she put it, "looking like a garage", says she hopes her arresting debut on the TV talent show will remind people not to judge by appearances.

'Ms Boyle, 48, from Blackburn, West Lothian, who is now tipped to win the contest, said that she hopes her story will set an example to the nation. "Modern society is too quick to judge people on their appearances," she said. "There is not much you can do about it; it is the way they think; it is the way they are. But maybe this could teach them a lesson, or set an example."

'At the pre-recorded audition, broadcast four days ago, audience members laughed at the frizzy-haired, churchgoing Catholic who lives alone with her cat in a rundown council estate, when she said she wanted to follow in the footsteps of the West End star Elaine Paige. Nevertheless, she said, she was determined to show them she has what it takes. "What you do is ignore that and get on with your act. You have to," Ms Boyle said.

'Minutes later the audience were on their feet, applauding wildly after her soaring rendition of 'I Dreamed a Dream', from *Les Misérables*.

'Born with a learning disability, Ms Boyle dreamed of becoming a professional singer but in order to care for her elderly mother, Bridget, limited her efforts to the church choir and karaoke.'

The article described the incredible change in her circumstances. 'Today, she is a worldwide sensation, a clip of her performance from the show has been viewed almost 2.5 million times on YouTube, and made it on to the news schedules in the United States. Prior to her TV debut Ms Boyle, who is unemployed, spent her days shopping, doing her housework, and occasionally visiting one of her eight siblings. Overnight she has become a national celebrity but is determined not to change.

'"I've had people recognising me, but I have gone on as normal – I am very down to earth," she said.

'Her ambition is to see her name in lights in London's West End. "It is early days yet," she says, but hints that there may already be a deal in the pipeline. "Baby steps," she replies, when asked if she has had any offers.

'She believes her age and life experience is her biggest asset: "It gives you faith in your abilities," she said. "I think I am ready for it."'

CHAPTER FOUR

MAKING THE
HEADLINES

Susan Boyle 'looked like a garage' when she appeared on *Britain's Got Talent*.

It was a devastating verdict on a middle-aged woman, a cruel comment to make, harsh, uncaring and insulting. It wasn't even a particularly good simile. Susan was hardly likely to take exception to it, however. She was the person who said it. She had actually watched the show when it was finally transmitted in her council house in Blackburn.

'They say TV makes you look fat and it certainly did. I looked like a garage. It was mortifying to see and a bit of a shock. I didn't realise I could reduce people to tears and I hope it wasn't because of that. I'm proud to be part of the show. It really is a dream come true.'

Then she made a telling remark, similar to ones that many others were to make in the ensuing mayhem, yet all the more insightful given that it was she who was making it.

'Modern society is too quick to judge people on their appearances. There is not much you can do about it; it is the way they think; it is the way they are. But maybe this could teach them a lesson, or set an example.

'What you do is ignore that and get on with your act. You have to. I like the way I am just fine. Why should I change a thing? It is my singing voice that matters first and foremost. I know there has been a lot of talk about the need for change, but my singing is the only thing that matters right now. Appearance is not everything – I am happy with the way I look.'

By the time she made these remarks, Susan had already received a standing ovation when she walked into her local Catholic church for Easter service. 'It was incredible. Although we sing in church, not a lot of them knew how good I was, so it was a bit of a shock to them. I'm a bit shy and retiring so they would never have known. It was very emotional. Everyone is very nice and it's lovely when all the kids stop me in the street to congratulate me.'

'I've had people recognising me, but I have gone on as normal – I am very down to earth,' she said.

'I'll get used to the fame side of things with baby steps – one step at a time. I am enjoying it very much just now. It's very good. I'll take the fame in my stride.'

She would have to, for now that the initial astonishment at her performance was over, the assessments began.

In any analysis of Susan Boyle and the impact she made, not just on television or show business but on society as a whole, it is necessary to examine in detail the reaction to her appearance and performance that Saturday evening.

The media do not always 'get it right'. In fact, they quite often get it wrong. But that cannot be said to be correct in Susan's case.

To be successful, and true to the public, they have to reflect the interests of those who read, watch or listen to them. So the reaction to those few minutes on a Glasgow stage was, in fact, a gigantic echo of the sentiment that was already building up in the public's mind.

A *Sun* writer said in one tribute: 'I send this message to the one and only Susan Boyle: Don't sweat it, m'dear. Because the rest of us were simply mesmerised. Now, given the choice between reality shows as fake as a nylon fur coat, talent shows brimming with the talentless, and a fork in the eye, blindness wins almost every time.

'The exception being the blue-moon occasions when the cynical millionaires behind these humiliation-based circuses of hate get it right. And it superglues you to the couch... And now, on the screaming train-wreck that is *Britain's Got Talent*, we have Susan. A woman who *is* reality TV. Because she *is* an ordinary person doing something extraordinary.

'Untouched by human hand, this girl. Literally. Kicking 50, never had a boyfriend. Eyebrows you could knit into a jumper, dress sense nicked from the drag queens on the paper towel adverts. But the voice? Borrowed from heaven itself.

'As little angels carried each note from her tonsils on velvet pillows, here – at last – we had found what shows like these were created for... Susan Boyle has a genuine gift that would never have been heard out with her own church hall but for this programme.

'The combination of her look and sound takes us back to the days of *Opportunity Knocks*, when it was what you did that counted, not what a wicked step-father had done to you.'

They went on to describe her in some ways as a throwback that should be celebrated. 'We should pray that her vocal cords stay healthy so she keeps on brightening Saturday night for millions. Most of all, we should hope she does so while remaining the person she wants to be... This lady, though, is who she is and the world should respect her for it.'

An opinion piece in the *Daily Express* continued the theme:

'The nation needed an Easter treat this year. Susan Boyle was that treat. On Saturday evening nearly 12 million people sat down to watch *Britain's Got Talent*. When she came on, multitudes would have yelled through their sitting room doorway: "Quick, come in and see this woman, she's fantastic." And a billion tears will have been shed. You didn't need Amanda Holden-style waterworks for this; everyone could do it (including your correspondent). If you missed Susan and you have internet, you can watch her on YouTube. By yesterday teatime 1,100,000 had. By now there will be many more.'

The article went on to describe the reaction of the judges. 'Simon Cowell's eyebrows rose an inch or two and he unleashed a gleaming white smile, Amanda curled her lip over her teeth and opened her eyes wider and Piers Morgan smiled broadly, and not in self-satisfaction. Within seconds the whole audience was on its feet, clapping and cheering. In the world of *Britain's Got Talent* they don't react, they overreact; they don't breathe, they hyperventilate. This time overreaction and hyperventilating were very much in order.'

And of her song choice: 'Her choice of song had been perfect... one of those mock-operatic numbers that gave her voice the chance to knock your socks off.

'The lyrics about forlorn hope meshed movingly with the woman singing them – 47 years old but looking older, clearly not terribly attentive to making the most of her appearance, unemployed, has spent years caring for her mother who died two years ago, leaving her devastated. Sounds sad, doesn't it? But I think we know she isn't.

'She's funny. Introducing herself to the judges, she says she's 47, then does a little shimmy and adds "that's just one side of me". A devout Catholic though certainly no church mouse, she's a performer.'

The article continued: 'Some contestants are very gifted, some up to a point; others are ridiculously untalented and often ridiculous in other ways too. Some are just tragic. Because Susan Boyle is no beauty, because she is not young, because she is single and spent her life with her mother in one of Scotland's less scenic villages, you might have thought she was being wheeled on as one of the tragic or at least tragic-comic. For the audience there was a "Heavens, what's this?" moment.

'Then she opened her lungs and sang and everyone knew it was a "Heavens, listen to this" moment. For Susan, who said she wanted a career like Elaine Paige's, it must have been divine. For the rest of us, it was a double-value, double-take.

'With absolute impunity we could now admit our shallowness: confess that when we first saw her we thought she was going to be a joke because she was a plain-looking middle-aged woman who hadn't had her hair or eyebrows done.

'Now we can congratulate ourselves on rising above that. We really care only about how beautiful her voice is. Aren't we wise and good to understand so clearly and feel so strongly that talent is all and beauty is only skin deep? Doubtless there are quite a lot of other women in Britain who would amaze us with their singing if they got the chance, but that is not the issue. Susan Boyle is this week's sensation. She has stood on stage and had the pleasure of seeing an audience knocked sideways. She has witnessed Simon enthusing, Amanda emoting and Piers exaggerating. She has given us a moment to remember for some time and herself an Easter she will never forget.'

Even the *Daily Mail*'s acerbic columnist Jan Moir had to note:

'Susan Boyle, the Hairy Angel, looks incredibly familiar to me. Perhaps it is just because there are so many moustachioed women in my Scottish homeland? However, I do worry about Susan. Before and after her performance on *Britain's Got Talent* last week, she appeared emotionally fragile, to say the least. That hip-swinging dance for Simon! Her perverted desire to kiss Piers! Yet there is something about her voice that stirs souls. When she sings, she seems complete in a way that evades her in real life. It is quite a performance.'

It wasn't just the popular press who had taken notice of Susan, however. *The Times* said: 'Susan Boyle is the ugly duckling who didn't need to turn into a swan; she has fulfilled the dreams of millions who, downtrodden by the cruelty of a culture that judges them on their appearance, have settled for life without looking in the mirror.

'This is a huge constituency, and it is weary of being disparaged. Women need an avenging force like Susan Boyle. No matter how brave, strong or resourceful they are, they get punished for not being glamorous; for being ordinary; careworn. At best they are treated as if they are invisible, at worst they are regarded as freaks.

Which is what the TV audience did with Ms Boyle until she started to sing.'

The 'bible' of the left-wing intelligentsia, the *Guardian*, had its own view of the sensation. And they put into print both what many felt and raised points many others were to raise in the ensuing months. Writer Tanya Gold poised the question:

'Is Susan Boyle ugly? Or are we? On Saturday night she stood on the stage in *Britain's Got Talent*; small and rather chubby, with a squashed face, unruly teeth and unkempt hair. She wore a gold lace dress, which made her look like a piece of pork sitting on a doily...Why are we so shocked when "ugly" women can do things, rather than sitting at home weeping and wishing they were somebody else? Men are allowed to be ugly and talented. Alan Sugar looks like a burst bag of flour. Gordon Ramsay has a dried-up riverbed for a face. Justin Lee Collins looks like Cousin Itt from *The Addams Family*. Graham Norton is a baboon in mascara. I could go on. But a woman has to have the bright, empty beauty of a toy – or get off the screen. We don't want to look at you. Except on the news, where you can weep because some awful personal tragedy has befallen you.'

After criticising the judges' reactions, she continued, 'And then Susan sang. She stood with her feet apart, like a Scottish Edith Piaf, and very slowly began to sing. It was wonderful.

'The judges were astonished. They gasped, they

gaped, they clapped. They looked almost ashamed. I was briefly worried that Simon might stab himself with a pencil, and mutter, "Et tu, Piers, for we have wronged Susan in thinking that because she is a munter, she is entirely useless."

'How could they have misjudged her, they gesticulated. But how could they not? No makeup? Bad teeth? Funny hair? Is she insane, this sad little Scottish spinster, beloved only of Pebbles the Cat?'

The *Guardian* piece continued: 'I know what you will say. You will say that Paul Potts, the fat opera singer with the equally squashed face who won *Britain's Got Talent* in 2007, had just as hard a time at his first audition. I looked it up on YouTube. He did not. "I wasn't expecting that," said Simon to Paul. "Neither was I," said Amanda. "You have an incredible voice," said Piers. And that was it. No laughter, or invitations to paranoia, or mocking wolf-whistles, or smirking, or derision.

'We see this all the time in popular culture. Do you ever stare at the TV and wonder where the next generation of Judi Denches and Juliet Stevensons have gone? Have they fallen down a RADA wormhole? Yes. They're not there, because they aren't pretty enough to get airtime. This lust for homogeneity in female beauty means that when someone who doesn't resemble a diagram in a plastic surgeon's office steps up to the microphone, people fall about and treat us to despicable sub-John Gielgud gestures of amazement.

'Susan will probably win *Britain's Got Talent*. She will be the little munter that could sing, served up for the British public every Saturday night.'

The writer added: 'Look! It's "ugly"! It sings! And I know that we think that this will make us better people. But Susan Boyle will be the freakish exception that makes the rule. By raising this Susan up, we will forgive ourselves for grinding every other Susan into the dust. It will be a very partial and poisoned redemption. Because Britain's Got Malice. Sing, Susan, sing – to an ugly crowd that doesn't deserve you.'

An astonishingly accurate dissection of the events of the previous few days – or simply 'a different take' by the *Guardian* on what had happened? Even if the article had hit the nail on the head, or at the least touched on some dark feelings within many people, nothing could be done to stop the rollercoaster that was SuBo.

The *Daily Mirror* adopted a similar, if somewhat more punchy, approach:

'Just for a moment, let's switch the sound off. Let's not listen to Susan Boyle's glorious, heavenly voice. Let's just contemplate her friendly face, her cheeky hip wiggle, the twinkle in her eye.

'Even before she opened her mouth and let that beautiful sound pour out, Susan looked a darn sight more fun than the frozen-faced freaks who were judging her. Apparently Simon Cowell and Amanda Holden were surprised. How could anyone tell? What the *Britain's Got*

Talent judges were shocked by wasn't Susan's amazing musical gift. They were shocked by her appearance.

'Were you? Me neither. She just looked like a straightforwardly nice woman to me. A bit of a laugh, a pillar of her community, a decent person who looks after others for no other reason than she thinks it's right. Yet she was presented as a hopeless case. Look at her! A 47-year-old unemployed cat owner who wouldn't know fashion if it slapped her on the Hermès Birkin. She's a stranger to tweezers. She's "never been kissed".'

Again pointing out how different it is for women, the article went on to say: 'How dare such an unsexy female even get up on stage! It's an outrage! If she hadn't sung so wonderfully, who knows what would have happened? Susan might have been lynched. Or worse, stripped to her underwear and sent straight to Gok Wan.

'It's different for men. Think of Elton John, Barry Manilow, Meatloaf, Van Morrison, Phil Collins, Jimmy Ruddy Nail... even Michael Jackson. No one ever looked at them and thought, "There's no way that man can sing. He's not good-looking enough, the loser. Banish him!" But no woman gets to perform publicly unless she looks like Mariah Carey. If you're a female singer, you are required by showbiz law to appear sexy at all times.'

It wasn't just the national newspapers who had decided that there should be virtually no limit to their coverage of Susan; the provincial press too was simultaneously enthusiastically raving about her performance and questioning just why it had had such an impact.

'When Susan Boyle walked onto the stage at the *Britain's Got Talent* auditions, she was the complete antithesis of our image-obsessed world. Dressed in a dodgy gold dress, with bushy eyebrows and her greying hair longing to be styled and coloured, first impressions meant we all expected her to fail miserably,' said Wales' *Western Mail*.

'After all, it wasn't a surprise when the 47-year-old announced she was single, living at home with only a pet cat for company or that she'd never been married, never even been kissed. It wasn't really a surprise when she waffled on to Simon Cowell about where she lived, how old she was or even when she started, rather embarrassingly, nervously gyrating her hips. The looks from the audience and judges alike summed up exactly what we were all feeling at home – this woman may want to be a professional singer like Elaine Paige, but she didn't stand a chance, did she? After all, she just didn't look right so what chance would she have against the bevy of half-dressed beauties looking to charm the judges for the chance to perform at the Royal Variety Performance. But Ms Boyle – even her name isn't remotely showbiz or sexy – had a gigantic surprise up her rather old-fashioned shaped sleeve.

'And when she belted out "I Dreamed A Dream" from *Les Misérables*, we were all left gobsmacked.'

Much nearer to home, the *Evening Times* in Edinburgh said: 'Let's hear it for the misfits: a select band of people at least half a step out of synch with the rest of the world who with every word, deed and thought dare to be different. Best of all, they are as natural in quirks and foibles as the rest of humanity is not.

'People like Susan Boyle, who bravely took to a stage and was ready to be mocked and patronised by some pretty shallow, sharp-minded showbiz cookies backed by an audience ready for a lynching.

'At first it looked as if yet another lamb was being led to the slaughter: Simon Cowell rolled his eyes, Piers Morgan smirked and Amanda Holden set her face in pre-performance sympathy-mode. As the camera panned over the audience, the only things missing were knitting needles and a guillotine.

'Then the gloriously plain and perky Miss Boyle opened her mouth and the rest is, as the sheep might say, history.'

The article, not one that favoured *Britain's Got Talent* as a show, continued: 'It is marshmallow media for the unthinking – until the likes of Susan Boyle comes along and shatters the pre-packaged myth of good looks, sophisticated charm, wit and style. Just an ordinary, wee, middle-aged, never-been-kissed spinster in a baggy dress with a twinkle in her eye and a singing voice that could shatter glass and splinter pigeonholes.

'By the time she makes her next appearance I am in no doubt the style gurus will have set to work: the frizzy bob will have been softened, there will be a gown and girders to even out the lumps and bumps.

'What won't change is her aura of danger and anarchy: the spirit of individualism that sets Susan Boyle and her like outside of the herd.'

The newspaper added: 'If anything, Miss Boyle – I refuse to say Ms because Miss was made for her – is a parable of our blighted, anxiety-ridden, narrow-minded times...it is also where Susan Boyle's hidden talent lies. Not in a glorious voice singing its way from a brown paper bag...but to shock herded humanity out of complacency, conceit and self-deception.'

Newspapers and television and radio stations around the world rely for a vast amount of their information on agency reports; the wire services, as they were once referred to. The unsung heroes of the newsgathering process, they disseminate information locally, nationally and internationally. One of the leading agencies is the Associated Press, and in the middle of the crazy week that ensued after Susan's Saturday night performance they sent out several stories, one of which was headlined 'Singing "spinster" strikes chord in talent contest'.

Datelined 'Blackburn, Scotland', it said: 'Susan Boyle lives alone in a row house with her cat Pebbles, a drab existence in one of Scotland's poorest regions. She cared for her widowed mother for years, never married and sang in church and at karaoke nights at the pub. Neighbours knew she could sing, and now – what with

YouTube, Twitter and countless blog postings – just about everyone else does, too... When she mounted the stage for Saturday's broadcast, her frizzy grey-tinged hair curling wildly and a gold lace dress clinging unflatteringly to her chubby frame, Boyle looked the antithesis of the American idols Simon Cowell normally anoints. She was greeted with giggles from the audience and eye rolls from the notoriously acerbic Cowell. The audience chuckled in embarrassment as she wiggled her hips awkwardly.

'Then she opened her mouth... her soaring voice drew startled looks and then delighted smiles from Cowell and the other judges. The audience leapt to its feet to applaud. More than 11 million people watched Saturday's show, but Boyle's instant success is due as much to new media as to the power of television, with a clip of her performance posted on YouTube by the show's producers drawing nearly 13 million views. Not to mention the skilful packaging of the segment, a mini-opera of underdog triumph.'

The report added: 'Boyle herself seems ill at ease with her newfound fame. At her modest, government-subsidised home on Thursday, she seemed more at ease making tea for visiting TV crews than answering questions about her life. She did mug for the cameras, however, crooning into a hairbrush.

'"It has been surreal for me," Boyle told the AP. "I didn't realize this would be the reaction, I just went on stage and got on with it."

'"She is often taunted by local kids. They think she's an oddball, but she's a simple soul with genuine warmth," a neighbour was quoted as saying. "Not many people these days are devoutly religious or would spend their time devoted to their parents to the point they'd find themselves a spinster."

'Susan told the agency, "I can hardly remember what happened on the night as I had my eyes closed most of the time. It really didn't dawn on me what was happening."'

Perhaps the most famous news agency of all is Reuters, the organisation founded in the middle of the 19th century and synonymous with the dissemination of news about major world events.

So how could they not write about Susan?

The message they circulated to the world in the aftermath of her appearance was: 'A middle aged Scottish spinster with untamed hair and a plain-spoken manner has captivated millions of music lovers and confounded celebrity watchers with her rise to fame after appearing on a British TV talent show.

'Susan Boyle, at 47, became one of the world's hottest celebrities virtually overnight after her rendition of "I Dreamed a Dream" on *Britain's Got Talent* this month.

'She has appeared on *Larry King Live* in the United States and in countless newspaper and internet articles. The clip of her song has been viewed around 50 million times on website YouTube.

'But while most people see her story as a fairytale,

some say it casts an unflattering light on the public and its preconceived notions about beauty and fame. They argue that the reason Boyle, who lives alone with her cat, became the instant star she has was because she did not look or behave like a "typical" celebrity.'

That even an organisation as prestigious as Reuters should see fit to give Susan the accolade of a feature about her life and television debut is a mark of how far she had come in so short a time. And nowhere had that impact been greater than in America.

The 'story had become the story', in newspaper parlance. In other words, the amount of column inches and air space that Susan was generating was now being mentioned as newsworthy in its own right.

The *Independent* was one of the first to note the fascination in America with the tiny lady from West Lothian.

'It didn't take long. Just days after Susan Boyle caused a sensation on *Britain's Got Talent* she has conquered another media market far away from her home in Blackburn, Scotland. She may not be in Beatles territory quite yet, but America is going nuts for the lady.' Under the headline 'Just Who Is The Singer Susan Boyle?' the paper went on to record the interest of others.

'The *San Francisco Chronicle*: "Unless you live under a rock, you know about the Scottish woman who has taken the industrialised world by storm. CBS scored biggest. There on its *Early Show* yesterday was a bemused-looking Ms Boyle for a live satellite interview from her front room. Veteran London correspondent Mark Phillips had been dispatched to her local pub to gauge her popularity among the punters – they love her.

'"You have become overnight a worldwide star," CBS anchor Harry Smith gushed. "Do you understand that, do you understand what that means?" Ms Boyle, who also sang a few bars again for those American viewers who had not already heard her on YouTube, responded very simply, "It hasn't completely sunk in yet."

'The whirlwind may only just have begun. CNN was yesterday reporting that after broadcasting excerpts of Ms Boyle this week, it had been besieged by requests from viewers for more. It also said that it would be following up the CBS with an interview with her on its own daily breakfast show, *American Morning*, today."'

The *Independent* mused on why Susan had this appeal in the Land of the Free. 'It is a country that will respond always to any variation of the fairy tale where the apparently unprepossessing suddenly becomes pretty, from *Shrek* to *My Fair Lady*.

'Thus some of the excited headlines yesterday, including "The Moment an Ugly Duckling Became a Swan" in the *New Jersey Star Ledger* and "Susan Boyle Stole My Heart" in the *San Jose Mercury News* in California. Stepping back a little, the *Daily News* in New York noted, "Susan Boyle was the Golden Ticket to Reality TV."

'"The grand prize for any 'reality' TV show is to stumble, with no prior warning or expectation, on to a moment of drama so engaging we would only expect to find it in carefully scripted fiction," the *Daily News* wrote. "That's the prize the British competition show *Britain's Got Talent* won last Saturday night when a rather drab-looking 47-year-old woman named Susan Boyle sang a version of 'I Dreamed a Dream' and stopped the show."'

The *Daily Mail*, too, recognised the global appeal the Susan now had.

'She is the most unlikely of showbusiness sensations. But amateur singer Susan Boyle has become an international star since wowing the judges and viewers of *Britain's Got Talent* six days ago. Show creator Simon Cowell is predicting a number one album in the US for churchgoer Miss Boyle after announcing that Oprah Winfrey, America's leading talk show host, had asked her on to her programme. This comes after 48-year-old Miss Boyle – who lives alone with her cat Pebbles for company – was interviewed for top US breakfast show *Good Morning America* yesterday.

'She has also been featured in newspapers around the world, even making the front page of the prestigious *Washington Post* and being described by another as having the "voice of an angel".

'Yesterday, appearing on *Good Morning America* by satellite from Britain, Miss Boyle was asked by host

Diane Sawyer if she wanted to change the way she looked. "I'd like that," Miss Boyle replied, adding, "I can't really believe this is happening."'

The *New Zealand Herald* said: 'A middle-aged volunteer church worker with the voice of an angel is Britain's latest unlikely showbiz star.' Even France acknowledged her talent when the French news agency AFP (Agence France-Presse) reported on her 'stunning musical debut'. Susan was truly on her way to becoming a global phenomenon.

CHAPTER FIVE

SUSAN GOES GLOBAL

One of the remarkable aspects of Susan Boyle's fame is how her appeal has transcended all nationalities and classes. She isn't just for the section of the public known, for better or worse, as 'the masses', or the various outlets of the media who constantly feed the outside world with information and tittle-tattle. Even 'celebs' themselves have fallen under her spell. And it didn't take long for that to happen, either. In the global village we all now inhabit, word circulated in a matter of days.

It was fitting that among the first to acknowledge her gift was Elaine Paige, the woman who had so inspired Susan throughout the years. 'I did not see the broadcast when it went out as I was taking a little break,' she said. 'But when I got back from that holiday my email box was inundated with friends telling me to watch the YouTube clip, which I did – along with everyone else in the world.'

The obvious question, given Susan's professed

admiration for Paige, was did the West End star think the Scot was any good – and was there a similarity in their voices?

'When I first saw the YouTube clip I remember having an idea in my head, "Oh, that's a voice I kind of recognise a bit." I think there is a kind of similarity. It has a tone to it, a similar timbre. Yes, I can hear a similarity, most definitely. It's slightly uncanny and a bit spooky even. Yes, I can hear it.

'When I saw her I thought she was wonderful. She has a clear, natural voice and I was blown away like everybody else. Hearing her sing with such freedom, it was an outstanding performance. When I saw her on YouTube and heard her say that she wanted to sing like me, I was very honoured and flattered. To be an inspiration, when you are completely unaware of it and then to discover in this way, is a, is a big surprise. Well, it's just very flattering.'

Paige thought Susan was a role model for other people who were dreaming of the same thing and, like many, found it refreshing to hear a voice that didn't belong to someone of 25 or younger. 'I think everyone is tired of that youth culture. Equally, in days gone by opera singers could be any shape or size or whatever and no one would comment on their appearance. It was their voice that mattered. I think it is the same with Susan. I think it is her voice that is her talent and I think she should stay true to herself. She comes from a little village in West

Lothian in Scotland; she is a country girl I suppose you could say. I think for her to be glitzy and glamorous in some village in Scotland is not the way for her to go about things and would perhaps be a little unsettling.'

And of the suggestion that the two should sing a duet: 'If it's something that Simon Cowell would like to do then it would be my great pleasure to sing with her. Of course, to be in the theatre is a whole different ball game. You need to sing eight times a week, you need energy and stamina and some training. I would love to meet her and talk to her and maybe have tea or something.

'She is a very natural girl you can see that in her performance. She reached out to the world, as it were. She's a country girl. And I think she just has the most lovely, natural voice. She's very open in her performance. And I think, you know, in such gloomy times that we're all sort of living through at the moment, economically speaking anyway, she was a breath of fresh air, and just came out of the blue and reached out to everybody.'

The star even had a message for Susan: 'If you want to sing together – let's.'

Days after being an unknown and generating a million smirks and eye-rolls with her ridiculous suggestion that she would 'like to be like Elaine Paige', Susan had the superstar herself not just coming out with a few polite words of praise, but a fulsome, generous and spot-on assessment of Susan and her appeal. And she wanted to sing a duet!

There was more praise to come Susan's way from another singer familiar with 'I Dreamed a Dream'.

The two words most often placed before Patti LuPone's name are 'Broadway' and 'Diva', and with very good reason. The singer, a contemporary of Elaine Paige, had a career which in many ways mirrored the Brit's: she starred in *Evita* and *Sunset Boulevard* and, most relevantly as far as Susan was concerned, in 1985, she created the part of Fantine in the Royal Shakespeare Company–Cameron Mackintosh production of *Les Misérables*. In recognition of that debut performance with the Royal Shakespeare Company she became the first American actress to win an Olivier Award.

She too was enraptured by Susan.

The two 'came together' on a CBS television show in America: Susan from the front room of her home in Blackburn, Patti on the telephone in the States. Standing ramrod straight in her small living room with its cheap-looking furniture and reproduction paintings on the walls, Susan, wearing a plain white dress and a chunky pearl necklace, answered the by now familiar questions about her performance and the reaction to it, before singing, at the interviewers' request, a few bars of the song.

Across the other side of the Atlantic, Patti LuPone was listening and she immediately said, 'I heard that, I cried. Susan, you got pluck girl. It's not an easy song, it's the ending actually that is the roughest part, as Susan will attest I'm sure. What you have to hit at the very end of the song that is difficult. It's an emotional song. It's the first ballad in the musical and it comes very early in the show. I saw her performance on YouTube like everybody else. Someone that works in my press agent's office in New York sent it to me, was it yesterday or the day before, I believe the day before yesterday. My husband and I watched it and I started to cry. Susan you made me cry.'

Asked how she rated Susan's rendition, LuPone said, 'From what I could tell on YouTube it was pretty great. So I can imagine what it was like live or on British TV. You can't really tell a lot from YouTube, but it was pretty powerful. I started to cry. I thought Susan has so much courage and so much pluck.'

The 'SuBo effect' worked for Patti too. Susan's version of the song had the knock-on effect of boosting sales of LuPone's original recording and putting it in the charts. LuPone wasn't the only *Les Misérables* 'old hand' who was enchanted.

Alain Boublil was the librettist on the original French production of *Les Mis*, which he co-wrote with composer Claude-Michel Schönberg. 'You expect nothing, and then she opens her mouth and you get three or four of the most exciting moments I have ever seen on television,' he said. 'I think of Edith Piaf. Piaf was a small woman who looked like nothing. And then she opened her mouth, and this beautiful sound came out.'

Boublil, who also wrote *Miss Saigon*, said of that YouTube appearance:

'Act I: She arrives and everyone is laughing at her. Act II: She bowls them over. Act III: Everyone is out of their seats.

'You cannot plan any of that. My wife was crying when she saw it. Even the most cynical people I know have been moved.'

'I Dreamed a Dream' was one of the first songs Boublil wrote for the musical in 1979. 'I remember I was in a car driving in the north of France and was working on this song about Fantine. Her descent into hell – she loses everything: her money, her daughter – takes up several chapters. I had to encapsulate 50 pages of the novel into a three-minute song. So I decided rather than to list all the happiness, I would go inside her head – "I Dreamt of a Different Life" was the original title. And that is how the lyric was born.'

The song was changed to 'I Dreamed a Dream' with the help of British lyricist Herbert Kretzmer, and Aretha Franklin and Neil Diamond's versions were among the composer's favourites.

Patti LuPone's version had just entered the charts at No. 27 thanks to the public downloading the song. 'I didn't even know the single still existed. The funny thing is that on iTunes, before you come to "I Dreamed a Dream," all the songs are hip-hop and dance records. *Les Misérables* is something quite special. Every time we think we are done with it, we are not,' Boublil said.

Neither was the public. Over 50 million people had

paid at the box office to see the show, translated into 21 languages, in practically every country in the world – 53 productions had been seen in 38 countries – producing takings of an estimated £1 billion. Opening in 1985 and still running, it was the longest-running musical production in the West End and there had been four different LP versions as well as numerous orchestral recordings.

No wonder Sir Cameron Mackintosh, the producer who first brought *Les Misérables* to the stage, said, 'I think there's every chance Susan Boyle will have the number one album in America, I will predict that. I was gob-smacked by her powerhouse performance. Vocally it is one of the best versions of the song I've ever heard.'

Susan's girlhood idol had been Donny Osmond. She still had some of his pictures on her bedroom wall, so it was fitting that he too should sing her praises.

Osmond sent a message of support telling how his wife wept as she watched and listened to Susan. 'I consider it an honour Susan used my songs to learn how to sing. Her success story is one that touches each one of us to be great against all odds. It's phenomenal what can happen today. Susan Boyle is the perfect example of that. When she walked out I was as cynical as everyone else. I thought, "This is a joke." But when she opened her mouth an angel came out. I looked at my wife and she had tears in her eyes. I got chills. She turned the world around in 20 seconds.

'I started hearing her say, "Donny Osmond is the inspiration behind my singing". It is unbelievable. I am so honoured to be considered her inspiration.

'I am so proud of you Susan for going out there and turning everybody around. You just keep proving them wrong.'

He was even to suggest recording a number with her – his classic 'Puppy Love' altered to 'And they call it, Susan love.'

'I would die to do a duet with her. I would have her come on stage and I would sing to her and she would sing to me. It would have to be "It Takes Two Baby." I would have to get rid of the vibrato though; I'm a little bit rock and roll and she's a little bit opera. I think everyone in show business should go out of their comfort zone, so you should take it to another level Susan, but don't lose that innocence.'

His sister Marie Osmond echoed his views. 'I think Susan is phenomenal. I love that you don't have to be this typical Hollywood stereotype – and people love her for that. She says that she used to lock herself in her room and look at Donny's pictures while she was singing.

'I just wish Susan all the best. I say "go girl and enjoy." Be yourself and have fun.'

In a world where the established means of communication such as newspapers and television seemed almost primitive, Susan was being transformed into a superstar by new technology in all its facets.

Television had launched her, it is true, but it was the relatively newcomer YouTube that literally overnight made her a name and an instantly recognisable figure globally. And the social networking website Twitter was to play its part, too.

The most followed user of Twitter in the world is reputed to be the American actor Ashton Kutcher and immediately Susan's YouTube clip was shown, he raved on Twitter: 'This just made my night.' His wife replied: 'This just made my night.'

His wife just happened to be actress Demi Moore, star of *Ghost*, *Indecent Proposal* and *A Few Good Men*.

Over 1.5 million people 'follow' the couple on Twitter and thousands of them clicked on the links. Within 72 hours of the original broadcast, four million people had watched 48-year-old Susan's performance. A show source said, 'Thanks to Demi's posting, Susan is now a genuine global megastar.'

As cast recordings of versions of *Les Misérables* entered the download charts as a result of the impetus Susan had given, she was given the good news about the 'endorsement' by the A-list Hollywood couple. It didn't make too much of an impact on her. A friend said, 'Susan had no idea who Ashton Kutcher was. Although she'd heard of Demi Moore, she didn't really know who she was. When I explained she was shocked and extremely grateful for their support.'

Susan also became a highly prized interviewee. CNN's

SUSAN BOYLE - LIVING THE DREAM

Larry King was more used to questioning Presidents and State leaders then Scottish singers, but soon he was talking live to Susan on his top-rated show. Also in on the conversation was Piers Morgan.

King asked: 'How did you feel, by the way, Susan, when you came onstage?' And she told him: 'It felt very daunting at first, but I gradually picked up enough courage. I was very confident with the title.'

King then said: 'Now, people laughed, though, when you walked out. Some even rolled their eyes, they made faces, who was this lady? Didn't that hurt you a little?'

'That didn't bother me because I knew I had to get on with my act,' Susan replied.

'So you had no question about your singing?'

'Well, I wasn't sure how I would be received so I just thought I'd give it a whirl.'

Larry King then brought Morgan in. 'All right. You're a judge, Piers Morgan. What did you make of this whole thing?'

'I sort of feel like apologising to Susan,' Morgan said. 'Since Susan, I know you're listening, I'm sorry, because we did not give you anything like the respect we should have done when you first came out because it had been a long day in Glasgow, in Scotland, and lots of terrible auditions, and then you came out and we thought you were going to be a bit of a joke act, to be honest with you. And then I can remember every time I watched a clip it takes me back to that second when you had begun to sing, and I had never heard a more surprising, extraordinary voice coming out of somebody so unexpected.'

He added: 'But what's astounding is the speed and the breadth of her success. I mean, I've been getting calls today from China, from Russia, from Australia. All around America, all around Europe. Susan Boylc has gone from total obscurity in the space of five days to global superstar and that's just extraordinary. I think that within a year, whatever happens to Susan on the show, whether she wins or not, I think we're going to see a number one album around the world. I think you're going to see a world tour and I personally just want to say to Susan, thank you for coming on the show.'

Morgan spoke of her appeal. 'You know, the great appeal and charm of Susan is the way she is. The way she looks, the way she acts. And I would like to extend an invitation to you to have dinner with me in London, Susan.'

Susan accepted.

She even managed to sing 'My Heart Will Go On' from *Titanic* totally unaccompanied, causing battle-hardened King to smile and say, 'Amazing. You're not kidding. Sinatra ought to be reborn. Susan Boyle, thank you. Best of luck. You'll be singing for the Queen, Susan, I predict it.'

There's probably only one television host in the world who can 'outrank' Larry King – and Susan was destined to meet her soon, too. That person was, of course, Oprah Winfrey – not so much a television personality but a way of life in America. It is a measure of the fascination that Susan held for Americans, that all the major TV shows were scrabbling to have her on, and Oprah was no exception.

Her talk show was the most watched of its kind ever and had made Winfrey rich. Very rich. She has been described as the richest African-American ever and the most influential woman in the world. Not bad for a poor kid from Mississippi who became pregnant at 14 yet went on to become a billionaire famed for her philanthropy. Her support of Barack Obama played a major role in his rise to becoming President. An appearance on her show is the Holy Grail for many with films, records and books to promote. And yet she was after Susan.

A film crew from her show flew to Blackburn and Susan was to be linked from there to the studio in America. It was to be a special 'The World's Got Talent', displaying some of the acts from the 'Talent...' shows over the globe.

There was only one slight drawback. After her impromptu performances on other morning programmes and the Larry King show, she wouldn't be allowed to sing. The reasoning was simple: the *BGT* bosses feared the other *Britain's Got Talent* acts would feel she was getting 'special treatment' and would have an unfair advantage over them before the contest ended.

Susan was even barred from singing in The Happy Valley Hotel, as none of the potential finalists were allowed to sing in public. 'All of our acts are advised not to perform in public if they have got through to the next stages of the contest. We want them to be seen first and foremost on *Britain's Got Talent*' was the explanation.

Nevertheless, she did contribute something special to the show, Oprah and her team decided subtitles should be used to help the American audience understand Susan during the pre-recorded chat.

Susan wore some make-up and a touch of red lipstick, to go with her yellow blouse and a sand-coloured jumper. Asked by Oprah if she wanted a makeover Susan screwed up her face and said, 'It depends on what you mean by a makeover.'

When Oprah mentioned her new haircut and clothes, Boyle added, 'I did a bit. Just to tidy myself up like any other female would have done.'

As the studio audience laughed, Simon Cowell, who was a guest on the Oprah show in Chicago, chipped in, 'Very good answer.' He also said that when he first saw Susan at the audition, 'This lady came up, and I'm thinking; "This will take five seconds and I can go have a cup of tea."'

That changed when she began 'I Dreamed A Dream'.

'She knew we were going to have that reaction and just to see that look of satisfaction on her face midway through – it was one of my favourite moments,' Cowell said.

Susan said she was 'loving every second' of her new-found fame and it was 'like a dream come true'.

And it wasn't just show business celebrities who were enthusing over Susan. Prime Minister Gordon Brown was questioned about her by Kofi Annan, Ghanaian Nobel Peace Prize winner and ex-Secretary General of the United Nations.

He asked the Premier for the lowdown on the Scottish singing sensation after delivering a speech at the Adam Smith College in Kirkcaldy. The two men struck up a conversation as they headed to a reception and the first thing Mr Annan said was, 'So, tell me about Susan Boyle?' As the men walked side by side Mr Brown looked deep in thought as he told Susan's story to one of the world's most powerful men.

Annan smiled broadly as Brown told him, 'Well, it's absolutely amazing. This woman has come from nowhere and has become a celebrity all over the world. And she comes from a wee village in Scotland.'

Former Downing Street spin-doctor Alastair Campbell advised politicians to recognise her 'authenticity'.

In a post on his blog, Campbell said: 'If politicians tend to read the Sunday papers with a mix of horror and trepidation, one person who must read them week after week with a sense of his own skills in shaping the popular culture agenda is Simon Cowell. The overnight sensation that is Susan Boyle and her 25 million YouTube hits is the latest chapter in Cowell's story. If there is a lesson from her success for politicians, it is authenticity. It is the only communication that works.'

Scotland's First Minister Alex Salmond, who was also from West Lothian, sent a letter of support. The SNP leader said: 'Please accept my warmest congratulations to you for your stunning performance on the ITV show *Britain's Got Talent*. I would like to wish you the very best of success for the remainder of the competition and in your ambitions for the future.'

Emails from admirers in Australia, Canada and the United States were published on West Lothian Council's website. One fan from Pennsylvania wrote: 'Your town should look up to this wonderful woman and be so very proud of what she has accomplished.'

More and more assessments of Susan and her impact were being made. And each one seemed more complicated and highbrow than the last.

Dr Robert Canfield, Professor of Anthology at Washington University in St Louis, Missouri, published an academic essay about the Boyle phenomenon, entitled 'Susan Boyle And The Power Of The Moral Imagination'

'Buried within the human psyche are feelings, yearnings, anxieties too deep for words, usually,' he wrote. 'Always it is something outside ourselves that touches us, somehow, where we feel most deeply. At such moments we remember that we are humans – not merely creatures but human beings, profoundly and deeply shaped by a moral sensibility so powerful that it breaks through our inhibitors; it can burst out, explode into public view, to our own astonishment.'

Dr Canfield said, in response to emailed questions, that Boyle captured 'the hopes of a multitude.'

Her performance resonates with millions, he said, because 'most of us in our heart of hearts have severe doubts about ourselves. So when a Susan Boyle appears on stage before a clearly condescending audience in a society that can read class status in every move, the hairdo, the dress, she appears as a loser. And we feel for her. We see how precarious her position is, how vulnerable she is, and we feel for her,' he said.

'We can see in her an objectification of what we fear about ourselves. So when she comes forth with that voice, that music – as if we have discovered Judy Garland at the age of 47 – we are thrilled. She's going to make it, we think. She's going to win (!). And we unconsciously invest ourselves in her achievement.'

Patricia Williams, a professor of law at Columbia University in New York, likened Susan's story to the election of Barack Obama. 'Boyle's ability to up-end conventional preconceptions is akin to what the "black is beautiful" movement of the 1970s tried to accomplish: a debunking of surface-based biases in favour of deeper commitments to fairness, intelligence, courage, humility, patience, re-examined aesthetics and the willingness to listen.

'Dismissing her – or anyone – based on careless

expectations about what age or lack of employment supposedly signify is the habit of mind common to all forms of prejudice.'

As always, there are voices that go ever so slightly against the crowd – not always too tastefully, either. In one case it was *South Park*, the surreal and often crude, cartoon series that mentioned Susan in an episode in which the characters run off to Somalia to become pirates.

In a letter to his parents, Kyle's little brother Ike writes: 'Dear Mommy and Daddy – I am running away. I am sorry, but I can no longer handle the monotony of middle-class life. Everyone at school is a f**king idiot and if one more person talked to me about that Susan Boyle performance I was going to puke my b***s out through my mouth.'

That little dig was nothing, however, compared to the criticism Susan was eventually to receive from Sharon Osbourne, wife of ageing heavy metal rocker Ozzy Osbourne.

The former *X Factor* judge said Susan had been 'hit by the ugly stick', adding, 'I like everybody to do well. Even somebody that looks like a slapped a***. God bless her. It's like, "You go girl". She does look like a hairy a***hole.' Sharon added in a US radio interview: 'She is a lovely lady. You just want to say "God bless" and here's a Gillette razor. I didn't realise she had facial hair – I couldn't get past the Gene Wilder wig. God gave her talent. But he hit her with a f**king ugly stick.'

Ten days later Osbourne had to eat humble pie. She apologised on her Facebook and Twitter pages, saying: 'Susan Boyle is a lovely, gracious woman and I took advantage. I would never want to be responsible for hurting Susan. I apologise for getting a cheap laugh at her expense.'

If *South Park* and Sharon had been a little less than enthusiastic, the same couldn't be said of the world's leading cartoon series, *The Simpsons*.

The roll-call of the great and the good who have been mentioned or made animated appearances in the show is practically endless but includes Ringo Starr, Dustin Hoffman, Sting, Bob Hope, Tom Jones, Elizabeth Taylor, Meryl Streep, Paul and Linda McCartney, Elton John, Mel Gibson, Tony Blair and JK Rowling.

Now Susan was to join that company when she was mentioned in an episode called 'Springfield's Got Talent'. Homer Simpson tells a Simon Cowell-type character, who is questioning him, 'My name is Homer Simpson, I'm 39 and, well, I've never been kissed.' He adds, 'My dream is to become a great singer like Susan Boyle.' Unlike Susan, poor Homer was doomed to fail and his attempts at singing were met with a chorus of boos.

There was no booing to be heard back in the real world, however. By the end of that first week, six days after her first appearance, more than 26 million people had seen the YouTube clip, with the number jumping from 1 million to 5.5 million in just one 24-hour period alone at the start of the week , making it the most watched video on the site globally that week. During the week Susan gave over 60 interviews. There were a couple of places where she wasn't making comments on the events of that crazy week, however: Susan didn't have a Facebook account and as for Twitter – well, she'd never heard of it!

CHAPTER SIX

A WEE MAKEOVER

She might have the 'Voice of an Angel', but it would be extremely naïve if not totally inaccurate to attribute Susan's fame to that alone. It was also her appearance that had captivated the world. The contrast between a voice of such sweetness and purity and an appearance which had led her to be cruelly dubbed 'The Hairy Monster' was immense. And it would be hypocritical to pretend that this gulf between the two was not a key factor – if not the major element – in the interest she was generating.

So, what was the last thing she should do? Everyone seemed to agree that her appearance, while eyebrow-raising in the extreme, was one of her 'selling points' and that it should not be altered. Indeed, it was Susan herself who said, 'I know what they [the judges] were thinking but why should it matter as long as I can sing? It's not a beauty contest. Maybe I'll consider a makeover later on. For now I'm happy the way I am – short and plump. I would not go in for Botox or anything like that. I'm content with the way I look. What's wrong with looking like Susan Boyle? What's the matter with that?'

She added, 'I wouldn't want to change myself too much because that would really make things a bit false. I want to receive people as the real me, a real person.'

That curly hair, which looked unkempt at the famous audition, had been frizzy at school, one of the reasons for the bullying she received as a child. But it was part of her totally natural image. So was the dress she wore. She had chosen it a year earlier when she was a guest at her nephew Alan's wedding. Her niece Jacqueline Houston said, 'When she came on screen, I shouted, "That's the dress she got for my brother's wedding!" It must be her favourite dress – or "frock" as she would call it. It's typical of her thrifty nature.'

As the number of viewings of videos relating to Susan hit 100 million, Susan decided to do what so many had advised her not to – she had a makeover.

All those aforementioned *BGT* judges had said she should remain the same, Amanda Holden even going so far as to maintain, 'I won't let Simon make her go to his dentist. And I certainly won't be letting her go to his hairdresser. I think that she needs to stay exactly as she is. She needs to stay exactly as she is because that's the reason we love her. She just looks like anybody who could live on your street. The minute we turn her into a glamour-puss is when it's spoiled.'

A WEE MAKEOVER

The change, when it came, made headlines around the world. But, being Susan, this was not the kind of makeover seen on television: money no object, designer clothes, the trendiest hairdresser, the most expensive make-up. No, none of that for Susan. Ten days after the first *Britain's Got Talent* broadcast she was spotted near her home in a brightly coloured patterned dress and leather jacket after admitting: 'I will need to sort out my dress sense and my weight. It wasn't until I saw myself on TV that I realised how frumpy I was. It's not a big thing, but I will be doing a bit more exercise. When there is this much attention on you, you have to plan what you wear every day and look your best. I just want to look nice and smart.'

If that was not a serious change in its own right, there was more to come. As one headline writer wittily put it, as a play on words of the Van Morrison classic 'Brown Eyed Girl', 'Tonight Simon, I'm Singing "Brown Dyed Girl".' Susan had her hair not only styled but dyed, too. The grey hair was replaced with a deep brown colour and the entire treatment cost a mere £35. Mind you, she also paid £5 to have those eyebrows trimmed as well.

There are many famous and fashionable salons that she could have gone to for the revamp – perhaps a surreptitious visit to a smart unisex salon after the regular customers had left, or one with the full attendant publicity? Instead Susan went chestnut at the previously little, if not completely, unknown 'Miss Toner' salon in

Whitburn, near Blackburn, West Lothian, just south of the M8 motorway.

Not, perhaps, the most famous hairdressers in the world but good enough for Susan who did not want to even travel to Glasgow let alone London, and it was there that 45-year-old hairdresser Caroline Boyle, no relation, carried out the transformation.

She dyed and then cut Susan's hair before setting to work with straightening irons. Susan, who also had a facial, left the shop after being there for one and half hours and raced to a relative's car before being driven off.

A friend said, 'Susan went for a chestnut colour. Her hairdresser did not want to make any huge changes and said she'd prefer to work with what Susan has already got. She was in the shop on Tuesday to get her eyebrows done and was just the same as always. She's not changed at all.' Another local added, 'It's really good that Susan decided to keep using this place. She has a wonderful talent – but it's fabulous to see that she's still so down-to-earth. She just had a wee makeover. She'll never go all Hollywood on us.'

Caroline Boyle described it as a 'collective decision' between Susan, her family and the stylist to give her a new look. 'We decided to change her a lot was not a good idea – you know she's charming as she is – so we just trimmed it a little and put a little colour in, to take away the grey. I think the papers like to sell papers, so they say some horrible things, but it's not nice for her family to read those kinds of things, so I think that's why she had a wee, mini makeover – just to make her look her best, rather than change her.'

She went on to say that Susan enjoyed whiling away an afternoon at the salon. 'She was very relaxed and she commented that it was the most relaxed she had felt in a few days, so she just sat in the chair and enjoyed the chat, and enjoyed the wee transformation.'

The hairdresser said the locals knew of Susan's singing talent but had been 'blown away' by her newfound fame, and commented, 'I don't think there was a dry eye in Scotland when she sang.'

Although at one stage Susan covered her hair with a scarf, the news was out – and it made newspaper and television headlines throughout the world: SuBo has had her hair done.

London's *Evening Standard* worried in a leader on the opinion pages: 'Oh no! She has only gone and had her hair done...Susan Boyle was at the centre of controversy today after paying £35 for a hairdo...It is a risky ploy for Ms Boyle, whose winning formula appeared to be based on her angelic voice and, what might kindly be put, her "organic" presentation.'

Another London paper said: 'She defied judges and showed off a new look and revamped wardrobe. She had her grey hair cut and coloured for £35 and her eyebrows reshaped for £5 at the Miss Toner salon in West Lothian. Despite concerns her new look would upset the judges, a show spokeswoman said: "Susan's a grown woman and can do what she likes."'

There was more to come. The transformation was not complete and soon Susan was spotted wearing a short, £16 imitation leather Primark jacket and a Burberry-style scarf, almost certainly not the real thing, when she was out and about. She also wore beige trousers and had a pair of slender spectacles on. There was even some foundation applied to her face and neck. This was big news.

The Scottish *Daily Record* said: 'Fans of Susan Boyle will do a double take when they see these pictures. She swore she didn't want a makeover, but two weeks is a long time in showbiz. Susan has undergone a remarkable trans-formation. First, the hair. Gone are the grey locks, replaced by a new chestnut brown, contemporary style. Next, the eyebrows. Skilfully shaped by waxing, they have changed the look of her face. Foundation and powder have taken the redness from her cheeks, giving her a more youthful look. Finally, she's ditched frumpy skirts for wide leg trousers and shirt, designer scarf, leopard print high heels and leather jacket. The overall effect is a younger, slimmer Susan with a look to match her voice.'

The *Scotsman* enthused: 'Draped in dowdy clothes, with hair askew and eyebrows like plump caterpillars, it was the contrast between Susan Boyle's unconventional look and her sublime voice that wowed the world. But now, as stardom beckons, the middle-aged spinster has spun a new style.

'In a makeover, the *Britain's Got Talent* contestant – who has attracted more than 100 million hits on YouTube – has exchanged the matronly flats for striking heels, cast off the cardigan for a trendy black leather jacket and dyed her grey hair chestnut brown. The eyebrows have been trimmed and tamed with the whole ensemble set off with the addition of a Burberry-style checked scarf. The 47-year-old's greying hair and plain attire have been the subject of intense debate across the country since her spine-tingling performance of "I Dreamed A Dream" earlier this month.'

Not everyone was pleased with the change, it said. 'It was reported that the makeover has caused consternation behind the scenes with sources on the show said to be "frantic", as they wanted to preserve her unique looks for the live finals.

'The contrast between Boyle's unkempt appearance and angelic singing voice is said by many to be the key to her meteoric rise to international fame. A neighbour said: "The TV folk might not like what she's done with herself. She looks really nice – nothing like the image that's had the whole world talking about her."

'One expert commented: "The shade of her hair could have been a bit warmer and the cut hasn't changed. Also, she has had far too much of her eyebrows plucked. If her clothes were that little bit softer, a bit more tailored, it would make a big difference. Having said that, it is obvious she has become much more aware of her image, and is trying to do something with it.'"

The *Northern Echo* also had its say: 'After a fortnight in which discussion of her looks has occupied as much newsprint and internet bandwidth as the Budget, singing sensation Susan Boyle appears to have caved in and undergone a makeover. The 47-year-old's greying hair and plain clothes have been the subject of intense debate across the country since her spine-tingling performance of 'I Dreamed A Dream', on *Britain's Got Talent*, but yesterday she was spotted outside her home in Blackburn, West Lothian, with chestnut brown locks and wearing a leather jacket. She also appeared to have had her bushy eyebrows trimmed.'

The *Daily Express* felt the change was so important it merited an item on the leader page: 'If Susan Boyle continues like this – kitten heels, new hair-dos, vampish lipstick – she won't be Susan Boyle any longer. It was her natural looks and honest demeanour as much as her voice that brought her fame. Her agent should remember what helped make her a star.'

In a separate piece, the paper also said:

'Susan Boyle's makeover will be an inspiration to many women because it is not only effective but remarkably cheap, proving you do not need a celebrity-style income to look good. Expect weight loss to follow and a diet book after that. Providing Susan does not let it all go to her head she has a career not just as a singer but as a beauty and fitness adviser, too. Good luck to her because she will need every ounce of that down-to-earth approach to survive the coming whirlwind.' The writer of those comments was Ann Widdecombe, the larger-than-life MP.

This being Susan Boyle, soon the news had travelled the world. And the debate as to whether she should have 'upgraded' herself was as fierce globally as it was in London or Scotland.

The *Sydney Daily Telegraph* – based 10,500 miles from Susan's home town – said: 'Singing sensation Susan Boyle last night revealed her new look – having ditched the dowdy appearance that helped make her an international phenomenon.

'The 47-year-old Scottish spinster – who has famously "never been kissed" – had her greying, frizzy hair dyed chestnut brown and styled… And instead of the old-fashioned dress she wore on the TV show *Britain's Got Talent*, Boyle was photographed wearing a stylish black leather jacket with what looked to be a Burberry scarf.

'In yet another sign she was raising her game in the style stakes, the reality TV contestant was wearing make-up and high heels. And Boyle – who was dubbed the "hairy angel" – had also had her bushy eyebrows plucked as well as a facial to brighten her skin. The makeover was revealed as she emerged from her home – where she lives with her cat – in Blackburn, Scotland.

'But her new look has caused consternation behind

the scenes with sources on the show said to be "frantic", as they wanted to preserve her unique looks for the live finals next month.'

That most cosmopolitan and energetic of cities, New York, wasn't immune to the SuBo effect either.

'Frumpy singing sensation Susan Boyle has once again shocked Great Britain – this time by swapping her homely gray-haired look for a salon makeover,' the *New York Post* reported.

'The Plain Jane singer has cut her bird's nest hair short and dyed it brown, along with getting a facial and plucking her beefy, mannish eyebrows. The new look made Boyle – who claims she has never been kissed – look more like her age of 48, rather than a washed-up old spinster. But the sudden styling has dismayed the producers of *Britain's Got Talent*, the TV show on which she made her stunning star turn earlier this month. They fear she may lose fans if she gives up her ugly-duckling image for a pop-star look.'

New Yorkers wanted to read and see everything they could about Susan, and the same applied to Californians. The *Los Angeles Times* asked:

'What's next, a fake tan? Britain is buzzing over singing sensation Susan Boyle's mini-makeover, with some worrying that her new look may cost her some support in the *Britain's Got Talent* competition that catapulted her to international stardom.

'Boyle, 47, became an instant YouTube and internet

celebrity after appearing on the British TV show with grey, frizzy hair, bushy eyebrows and a jowly face above a remarkably unflattering dress. The contrast between Boyle's unadorned looks and her angelic singing voice endeared her to viewers the world over.

'But Boyle has now appeared sporting freshly dyed and styled brown locks and newly shaped eyebrows.

'Though no one could accuse Boyle of turning into a WAG – as the highly stylized wives and girlfriends of England's wealthy athletes are called – the difference was shocking.'

The *Detroit Free Press*, based in the 'motor city', said: 'A well-known ugly duckling is getting some help becoming a swan. Susan Boyle became an international sensation when her recent appearance on *Britain's Got Talent* hit YouTube. The most polite term applied to her appearance was "unconventional", so it was hardly surprising that she emerged with a new look Friday.

'Her once grey hair is now brown and her thick eyebrows are considerably thinner. The frock she wore for her audition was replaced Friday with a more flattering ensemble that included a leather jacket.

'A prominent British publicist, Max Clifford, isn't a fan of the new Boyle. "Keep her as natural as possible for as long as possible," he says. "She has to make sure that the person people all around the world fell in love with remains the same."'

A Canadian paper had the headline, 'Whether she

should have or shouldn't have, she did', and everyone immediately knew who they were talking about. 'Susan Boyle has dyed and cut her frizzy, greying locks and thinned her famous bushy eyebrows, a US$57 sprucing up that has become huge news in Britain.

'On Wednesday, with the blinds pulled down at the Miss Toner salon to give the unlikely global celebrity a little privacy, Boyle got a haircut, semi-permanent colour rinse and eyebrow shaping, according to a receptionist at the Whitburn, Scotland, salon.

'Since she appeared April 11 on the television show *Britain's Got Talent*, her decidedly unglamorous looks have become a subject of global debate. Many of her fans urged her not to let stylists change her, while others advised her to pay more attention to her appearance.

'The *Sun*, the bestselling British tabloid, had dubbed her "Hairy Angel" but yesterday referred to her as "Brunette's Got Talent."'

'"I assure you it's not a major makeover," her brother John Boyle said. "She is still the same Susan." Boyle's show-stopping success has sparked a worldwide argument about the nature of beauty and celebrity. Her fans call her a refreshing change from the parade of airbrushed celebrities on the airwaves. Others have said that there's nothing wrong with maximising your looks, and that Boyle really ought to let the stylists release her inner princess. Online sites have run surveys and blogs about whether she should get a makeover.

DailyMakeover.com said 75 per cent said "yes" and that it would not "detract from who she is." Some online commentators had speculated that the talent show host Simon Cowell might forbid a makeover because it could kill the golden goose; the unvarnished Boyle is the biggest thing ever to happen to his television show.'

The *Globe and Mail*, often described as Canada's newspaper of record, commented:

'Last week, Susan Boyle got a bit of a makeover, and it sent some people around the bend. The breakout star of *Britain's Got Talent*, familiar to hundreds of millions of tissue-clutching fans thanks to that YouTube clip, has had a bit of fluffing. When she first appeared on the audition phase of the show a month ago, it was clear from Simon Cowell's look of disdain and Piers Morgan's wrinkled nose that here was an alien specimen: a 47-year-old woman in a mother-of-the-bride dress, with upper arms that swayed gently in the breeze, wearing not a stitch of makeup. Worse, perhaps, Boyle was a woman of hair. She was not, as women are supposed to be, as smooth as a Barbie fresh from the Mattel factory.

'Boyle will be back in the semi-finals of *Britain's Got Talent* in a couple of weeks. In the meantime, she's had a wee polish, as the folks in her town of Blackburn might say. It's nothing radical – she hasn't gone the whole Joan Collins, with a small, glossy mammal affixed to her head, or taken to the scalpel like Joan Rivers, so that her eyebrows orbit Jupiter.

'No, our sensible Susan – because we all feel we own a piece of her now – has put on a sharp leather jacket and a Burberry scarf, and taken the grey from her hair. Her eyebrows might have visited a trainer... This, predictably, has led some of her fans to cry treachery, as if by making herself more conventionally attractive, Boyle has undercut her authenticity. What cobblers! She's just following the same script that Hollywood (and now, London) has always provided women who need a bit of help in the glamour department.'

The article went on to say that Susan's journey was a familiar narrative, and that *Britain's Got Talent* was all about familiar narratives. 'People weep at the clip of her singing not because they feel sorry for her but because it's a reminder of every loser-makes-good, beauty-on-the-inside fairy tale we've ever been told, and want desperately to believe. Taking her out of that safe box marked "loser" dilutes the fairy tale a bit, but the box can't hold her forever... When Boyle sheds her frumpy cocoon, she's messing with the storyline. Good for her. The press in Britain will continue to call her "hairy angel", "47-year-old virgin" and "West Lothian spinster", but I sense that Susan's got a bit too much personality to lie still while the labels are affixed. There's a showgirl in there, and showgirls need sequins.'

Although she had stayed local for that first makeover, Mayfair stylist Nicky Clarke, whose clients had included Diana, Princess of Wales, singers George Michael and

David Bowie, actress Liz Hurley and many other stars, said he was due to have a consultation soon with Susan, pointing out, somewhat ungallantly, if the reports were accurate: 'At the moment she looks a bit like a man in drag, but there's a lot of potential there and when I've finished she is going to look really beautiful. I'm going to soften her hair with lowlights, which will freshen the face up. She will look stunning.'

No wonder Simon Cowell said he was fed up with stories about Susan's hair, eyebrows and cat and urged her to focus now on winning the television talent competition.

'She has got four weeks to prepare for the biggest night of her life, and she has got to sing better than she sang before with all those expectations on her. But it could all go horribly wrong for her because there are so many other distractions,' Cowell told TV reporters in Los Angeles. 'Get yourself together sweetheart for the big one – the semi-final. Shut the door, choose the right song and come back as who you are, not who you want to be,' he said.

Another, although somewhat different word of caution, came from Susan's brother Gerry, who reckoned that his sister should capitalise on her new-found fame. 'There is a public appetite for a single but no product for people to buy. *BGT* need to step in and sort this out. The silence coming from *BGT* is causing a frenzy. We are all getting sucked into it and it's getting a bit much now.' And he warned, 'When I last spoke to Susan she sounded exhausted. I said, "How are you?"

and she said, "Oh Gerard, I've been here there and everywhere." She's been up and down to London for meetings with Sony and I could tell she was shattered. I said to her, "Get off the phone and get to bed. You need to rest."'

Gerry added, 'Susan is frustrated. She's not thinking about big cars and Bentleys. All she wants to do is sing, but she's not being allowed to do that. The pressure would be much less and the whole thing much better if there was a management team to look after her.

'She's normally oblivious to what's going on around her. But now she's realising, "Why can't I do this, why can't I do that?"'

He even said all the attention meant that Susan had not been able to attend mass at her church. 'I have stayed away from what used to be our family house because there's so many people camped out there. It's been like a scene from the film *Notting Hill* every time she opens the front door.' Susan had to go to her sister's home in Motherwell at one stage to escape the media frenzy, although she had no plans to move permanently from her own home.

'I know Susan thinks she's staying in that house to her dying day but someone needs to step in and do what's right for her.' He added, 'Is there a management deal or not? I imagined Cowell would move forward on this. But she's got too big for the show.

'We've got a star on our hands and the appetite for her

first record is huge. From a business point of view they are not capitalising on her success. Any established act would love to crack America, but Susan's done it in eight days. So do we keep on going and take up these offers or – for the good of the show – do we ignore the fact everyone is baying for a product?

'They can't just sit back and ignore this phenomenon just because she's a contestant.'

Susan's response to this, and to suggestions that she might leave the show as the pressure was by now too great for her was, 'There is no way I am quitting. The only way I'd leave the show is if Simon Cowell kicked me out.

'All I can promise is to do my best and confirm to everyone that I'm not leaving the show.'

She had to admit, however, that life was now hectic. 'I've been on American TV a lot and I've never even visited America. It's crazy.

'I would go, definitely, if that's what they want. I'm not changing my accent or anything. If I'm talking to people I don't know then I'll put my posh voice on. But I'm Scottish and there's nothing they can do about that. I've lived here all my life. I wouldn't want to move anywhere else at the moment.

'I usually sing a lot when I do the housework. But I have neglected my home a little bit – the house definitely needs a tidy. I will never be too famous to tidy my own house. I do my own cleaning, I find it very therapeutic.

'I didn't realise the attention would be on this scale. When I entered I didn't think anything would come of it. I never expected it to be so mad, but I am loving it. I will need a holiday after all of this is over.'

How fame is measured is a difficult question to answer in the modern world. One old standard that was used was simply the number of newspaper column inches a celebrity could tot up. The more inches the greater the fame. That was overtaken by how much airtime was devoted to them on television, and, in the past few years the number of hits generated on the internet, through YouTube, Twitter, Facebook and all the other social-networking sites.

But the growth of the 'celebrity magazine' added a new dimension. If you weren't in *OK!* or *Hello!* then you weren't a celebrity; it followed as surely as night followed day, didn't it?

So it came to pass that Susan Boyle, who had dreamed her dreams while looking into a mirror and singing into her hairbrush in her council home in West Lothian, was – in the breathless language so loved by the magazines – 'speaking exclusively to *OK!* about her sudden success and her secret kiss!'

She told the magazine:

'I wish I'd never said that I'd never been kissed – I only meant it as a joke! I have lived a life. They just don't know about it! There's plenty of time to find love. I'd like to visit America, but I'm a wee bit reserved about the men. I like to keep myself to myself. Being myself hasn't done me any harm so far. If you lose your identity you become something that's false and people stop believing in you. Why should I go for Botox and things like that? You don't need all that. If you can't be yourself then who can you be?'

There had been stories that a film of her life was being mooted, some reports even suggesting Catherine Zeta-Jones as a somewhat unlikely figure to play Susan. 'It would be a knockout if they made a film of me – but that's for the future. I just want to concentrate on the present. It's baby steps! I'll think about which actress I want to play me nearer the time!

'I would love to be in a musical or a film, but this is all too far off in the future. People used to tell me I should make my voice known to people – but I felt I wasn't mature enough to handle the attention. I'm strong enough to do it now. Finding the strength to cope after my mum died proved that to me. I hope my mum is proud of me now. It's all for her, my family and the people who support me.'

CHAPTER SEVEN

THE PRESSURE
MOUNTS

BBC Radio 4's *Today* programme, broadcast every morning from Monday through until Saturday, is an institution. The long-running current-affairs programme is the most listened to on Radio 4 and its influence is immense. It has the latest on the day's news, covers breaking stories throughout its time on air and delivers in-depth interviews with leading figures. It has more than six million listeners, a massive number, and is widely considered to be the most influential news programme in Britain. The size of its audience isn't the only barometer by which its impact is measured either; its demographic also forms a key part of its influence – it is the movers and shakers' 'must-listen' radio.

One of its regular features is Thought for the Day. Many of those who give this brief talk on a theological matter have become household names, most notably Rabbi Lionel Blue and Richard Harries, the former

Bishop of Oxford. The talk has an ancestry that predates the programme itself; a religious topic has been discussed on the network, including its predecessor the BBC Home Service, in roughly the same breakfast-time slot since 1939. Its speakers are normally Christians, but many other religions have been included, too.

On 23 April the speaker on Thought for the Day was The Reverend Angela Tilby, vicar of St Benet's Church in Cambridge. And she discussed Susan Boyle. She didn't just mention her in passing either; she actually compared her *Britain's Got Talent* appearance and the reaction to it with the impact Jesus would have had on those who came to hear him speak. No matter how valid or tenuous the connection, her impact was now being compared with the son of God. Yes, it was getting this serious.

'The odd thing,' Reverend Tilby remarked, 'is that what was so moving about her performance was the sheer dissonance between face and voice. People assumed that because she was not glamorous she couldn't have talent. Yet in the midst of the catcalls she simply said, "I'm going to make this audience rock". And she did. She had real authority. Authority is a strange word to use in this context, but that is what I saw when I watched her on YouTube.

'It has reminded me bizarrely of the way the Gospels speak of Jesus. On the one hand they claim he had an authority which was utterly convincing. Yet at the same time he is identified with the broken figure from the book of Isaiah. One with no beauty that we should desire, despised and rejected of men, one from whom men hide their faces.'

It was a remarkable comparison to make, and as *The Times* noted: 'This is a pretty hefty burden to place on Boyle's shoulders.' An understatement if ever there was one. To compare her impact with that of Christ's, where was it all going to end?

As far-fetched as some thought the comparison was, at least it was an observation delivered with love and goodwill as its central theme. The same could not be said of another reaction to one fleeting fragment of that historic appearance.

While Susan had been talking to the judges prior to her audition song, the cameras had flitted across the faces of those in the audience. Slouched low in one of the theatre's seats was a pretty young girl who, like so many around her, looked both surprised and dismissive, her slight rolling of the eyes showed that she was both amused and disbelieving.

Yet her innocent reaction was to make her the subject of a hate campaign that was to be labelled 'internet fascism'. A clip of Susan's *BGT* audition had provoked a host of abusive and threatening posts against the teenager, nicknamed the '1:24 girl' because she appears just under one and a half minutes into the clip.

One read: 'Talk about never judging a book by its

cover. [By the way], anybody else feel like punching the chick at 1:24 in the face?'

'Not enough has been said over her: the girl at 1:24,' adds another 'Can we not find her and name and shame her, please? She leaves a bitter aftertaste in my mouth.' Friends of the teenager even said the show's producers singled her out in the editing of Susan's performance and that the young woman was 'extremely upset' by the campaign, adding 'everyone in the venue was in exactly the same boat, booing Susan and heckling her before she had even begun to sing.'

Susan sprang to her defence. 'Leave the poor girl alone,' she said. 'She had the same reaction as the judges and everyone else in the theatre; she does not deserve this treatment.'

The programme makers were concerned enough about the development to say: 'She shouldn't be a target and we would ask her to get in contact if she has any concerns.'

Eventually the girl was identified as Jennifer Byrne, 18, now a great fan of Susan's, who felt it unfair that she had her face shown on air. Hairdresser Jennifer said, 'It was a split-second reaction that changed my life. All I did was roll my eyes and I'm targeted by a hate campaign for months. I just can't believe how I have been targeted by total strangers around the world who don't even know what kind of person I am. I really didn't mean any harm. I think Susan's a fantastic singer who deserves all of her success.

'I've been pretty shocked by it all and I really just want it all to stop now. They could have filmed 100 people around me with exactly the same expressions.'

Twisted strangers had made contact with Jennifer's friends with messages like: 'That wee bitch will burn in hell' and 'Anyone smacked the bitch yet?'

'Going to the *BGT* auditions was supposed to be a great night out with pals,' Jennifer went on to say. 'I can't believe how it all turned out. What really bothers me is how the production company only kept in that split-second shot of me when there were hundreds of other people doing exactly the same thing.' Jennifer, who went with eight friends to the audition, added, 'We were quite near the front so we had a really good view. I knew that the camera was close by us, but as the night went on we forgot it was there because we were just having such a good time.

'When Susan came on, everyone in the audience thought she looked a bit odd, wiggling her hips to the judges. Everybody thought her audition was going to be a disaster – there had been some terrible ones earlier. All I did was roll my eyes the same as everyone else in the audience, including Simon Cowell. She just looked a bit out of place. Some people near us were shouting to her before she had even started singing. But when she sang, we all just jumped to our feet. And as soon as I got home I told my mum about this amazing singer and how she could probably win the competition. What really annoys me is that the producers didn't show me when I was up clapping and cheering Susan. It looks as though I didn't appreciate her, which is not true.'

Three months later, the programme was transmitted. 'We were all sitting watching it and then suddenly my face popped up. I couldn't believe it. All my pals started texting saying they'd seen me. But even then I said to my mum, "Why did they show me looking like that?" Within a few days people started messaging me on the internet with some really nasty stuff. They were saying things like "Let's get the bitch" and "We'll hunt her down and slap her". It was really upsetting to see such horrible things being said about you. Over the weeks and months it got worse and worse. One day I was on the train and somebody recognised me and started to try to film me on their mobile phone. It was pretty spooky. At one point my pal put a jumper over my head just to stop them.'

Poor Jennifer was even booed by the audience when the clip appeared on the Oprah Winfrey show in America. A Facebook page was set up by supporters of Susan in which Jennifer was criticised and the attacks continued on online forums.

Jennifer reckoned she was getting a much harder time of it than Sharon Osbourne, who had come out with a personal and vulgar attack on Susan. 'It's pretty shocking when you see the really horrible stuff she said and she escaped with a quick apology.' She added, 'It really meant a lot when Susan defended me. At least she knows I'm a big fan,' she told the *Sunday Mail* newspaper in Scotland.

One thing the campaign hadn't done was cause Jennifer to develop an aversion to *Britain's Got Talent*. 'I love all these kinds of shows. I've applied for tickets for the auditions in Glasgow again next year – but I won't be sitting anywhere near any cameras.'

Young Jennifer wasn't the only one caught in the wake of Susan's fame: an MP was forced into an embarrassing public apology after jokingly linking Susan's success with swine flu. Siôn Simon, Minister for Further Education in the then Department for Innovation, Universities and Skills made the 'joke' on Twitter, shortly before Prime Minister Gordon Brown announced details of British cases.

'I'm not saying Susan Boyle caused swine flu,' he said. 'I'm just saying that nobody had swine flu, she sang on TV, people got swine flu.' But he later apologised on Twitter, saying, 'Earlier I repeated a joke that was in poor taste, which I now regret. I apologise wholeheartedly for any distress or embarrassment caused.'

The public had taken to Susan in their millions, but that couldn't prevent some unkind people deriding her and her looks. On Graham Norton's chat show he and *Little Britain* star Matt Lucas both made unkind remarks about her and the ensuing publicity she had received.

Lucas joked about whether Susan was in a Top 100 sexiest women list yet, and then he said, 'She is definitely the best singer I have seen that looks like Bernard Manning.' Norton then added, 'For a hairy woman with thick ankles she is amazing. But as a singer she is just OK.'

Such was the attention Susan was attracting that she had to change her telephone number. A friend said, 'The past month has been manic and her house phone has been red hot. Because Susan has become an international star, she was getting calls in the middle of the night. Now she has a number which only relatives, close friends and producers have. It's fair to say Susan is a bit of a technophobe – she's never even used the internet. The show's producers have told her to use a mobile, but she doesn't have a clue how to, so never has it on.'

If Susan was aware of the cheap jibes of some comedians, she would have been comforted by words of praise from a fellow female Scottish singer. Aberdeen-born Annie Lennox was tall, angular and strikingly beautiful. She had also studied at The Royal Academy of Music before achieving fame through her vocals, first with the Eurythmics and then as a solo artist. She had sold millions of records and – with her sometimes androgynous appearance – had become a style icon. So, she knew what she was talking about when she said, 'This phenomenon with Susan Boyle. She's not a goddess to look at, God bless her. But everyone was deriding her and that's very cruel. And then she sang and they all give her a standing ovation. It's almost like the Romans where they put the thumbs up and you're the best and you can survive or they put the thumbs down and you're dead in the water. If people like your music you can't guarantee they're going to love you, they're going to hate you, you just never know. So you go along with the journey. You learn to be philosophical.'

Paul Potts, whose own story of success with *BGT* in spite of initial reservations about his appearance, echoed her thoughts. 'I think she's great. She's done really well and she's coped with the media attention incredibly. I don't know how I would have reacted to suddenly finding photographers outside my doorstep.'

It wasn't just singers who were on her side, either. The Golden Couple of the day were Manchester United and England star Wayne Rooney and his wife Coleen. So words of support from Mrs Rooney were akin to being granted a Royal Warrant.

'Susan Boyle is great and I had goosebumps when she sang. I was so pleased that she did well. The crowd didn't seem that supportive when she first came out on stage, but now the world loves her.

'Apparently over 100 million people have watched Susan's performance on YouTube, which is just amazing. Good on her, she deserves it. She's had so much attention and publicity, and I hope something comes of all this and that it lasts. I bet she'd be great in a musical – she reminded me of a drama teacher!

'I have to say that I do find it a little sad that people are saying Susan has to have a total makeover. I think it's up to her if she wants to have one or not. Every woman loves to have her style updated, but an extreme makeover shouldn't be pushed on her because she's been very successful with the way she looks now. I mean, she's just had her hair restyled and it looks good, but she shouldn't go too far as I think she's fab as she is. But every woman loves a bit of a makeover and I hope she enjoys getting pampered.'

With her new-found fame, many major businesses and companies were eager to be associated with her, a fact noted by the prestigious *Marketing Magazine*: 'A host of brands are vying to sign up *Britain's Got Talent* contestant Susan Boyle to promote their products.

'According to a spokeswoman for production company Talkback Thames "all imaginable brands" from sectors including hair-care, mobile, food, FMCG (fast moving consumer goods such as food and drink, perfumes and washing powders) and utilities have sounded out the talent show's producers. "We've been inundated with calls," she said.'

Despite the interest, however, Boyle, who has taken the show by storm, will not be able to sign any contracts until after the series ends later this month.'

That didn't stop one cheeky bar owner from promoting a cocktail he had named after her which was 'designed to be a little bit cheeky, just like she is...When you take a sip, it'll leave a little moustache.' The £9 cocktail contained vodka, wild strawberry and sour rhubarb liqueurs, blossom water, cranberry juice and mixed berries. When topped with a creamy Frangelico layer and sprinkled with chocolate shavings it's true that it would inevitably leave a slight 'moustache' on the upper lip of anyone who drank it!

Susan, not a drinker anyway, was too busy to try it; in early May she was showing the Oprah Winfrey film crew around her house so that they could prepare for her link with the talk-show queen during her 'World's Got Talent' series. The crew only stopped filming at one stage in the afternoon when they had to leave the house as Susan was 'having a nap'. Susan, who had been sporting a pink fluffy scarf, a turquoise blouse and even a touch of red lipstick, posed for a scene in which she welcomed them to her house and offered them tea and Scottish cakes.

Reference has already been made to that appearance – with Oprah and Simon Cowell assessing acts from around the world – but he summed up the show's appeal, to acts and public alike, when he said, 'It gives the underdog a shot, and I think it's brilliant. The fact that we're allowing the public to make the decisions most of the time is a really good thing. The great thing about it is when you start seeing it in places like China and Afghanistan. It's democracy. We've kinda given democracy back to the world.'

He was obviously, and understandably, proud of the programme. But there were others who were less kind with many critics in the UK pointing out the comparison between show's success and the fate of *The South Bank Show*, the television 'highbrow' look at the arts, and seen in 60 countries worldwide, whose forthcoming demise had just been announced. It attracted a million viewers compared to *BGT*'s ten million-plus. But even Melvyn Bragg, the programme's elegantly coiffured presenter would not attack *Britain's Got Talent* or Susan – he too had fallen under her spell.

Having been told that his programme, which had been on air since 1978, was to end, Bragg, a Labour Life Peer, said, 'I later hear from an insider that the new budget would give an entire season of *The South Bank Show* about half as much money as is spent on one episode of *Britain's Got Talent*. Of course, *The South Bank Show* doesn't have anything like the pull of *Britain's Got Talent*, which is seen by more than 10 million viewers. An average *South Bank Show* gets one-tenth that audience. They say we only get a million. Well, for Christ's sake. Sky television would die for a million. A million people would fill up the Royal Opera House for two years! And if we were played at a regular time, regularly, and promoted, things might go up a bit. But never mind. A million is okay.'

And he pointed out, albeit obtusely, his liking for the Cowell show. 'I like pop culture, I liked it when it was

Opportunity Knocks,' he added, pointing out that he loved Susan's performance. 'And the Great Moment [Susan's appearance and song] is wonderful.'

Susan's appearance on the *Oprah* show meant that she had performed for the unofficial First Lady of America, but she was not going to say 'yes' to the First Man, President Barack Obama. There were numerous reports of her being invited to the prestigious annual Correspondents' Association Dinner in Washington DC. But she was said to be too nervous to accept the offer to be in the presence of not just the President but also a raft of celebrities at the Hilton Hotel. One source said: 'She was shocked and thrilled by the invite – but it was all too much too soon for her so she said "no". She has been told President Obama has seen clips of her on TV and loved her singing. And she is delighted. She knows she would have been incredibly nervous if she'd gone. But her dream is to sing for President Obama one day. She loves him and thinks he is already a terrific President.'

If it was the thought of those A-listers who might be there that was off-putting for Susan, a look at those who did attend confirmed their status. Singer Sting and wife Trudie Styler, actress Demi Moore and husband Ashton Kutcher – as we've seen already, big fans of Susan's – and TV chef Gordon Ramsay and his wife Tana were among the VIPs present. Also in attendance at the White House Correspondents' Association Dinner were Tom Cruise and wife Katie Holmes, Samuel L Jackson, Jon

Bon Jovi, Tyra Banks, Eva Longoria Parker and hero pilot Chesley Sullenberger who successfully landed his stricken passenger jet in the Hudson River in February.

They had to find a replacement for Susan, and beautiful singer Natasha Bedingfield filled the gap.

Perhaps there was one person better placed than anyone else to assess Susan's impact, her current position and what the future held for her. That person was Simon Cowell, and he spoke at length to the *Daily Record* about all these aspects of her life in the run-up to the week-long auditions that would decide who would make the final of the programme.

'It's early days, but Susan could become the biggest star I've ever discovered. She's got a real shot this year of doing something phenomenal for herself, probably more than she realises,' he admitted. 'I think every record label in the world would want to sign Susan right now. She is in a fantastic position. I have never seen anything like it in my life. Susan is the biggest entertainment story this year. It has dominated the news for weeks and never gone off the radar.

'It's the biggest phenomenon I've ever seen out of any of my shows. I've never seen anything travel so quickly, particularly what happened on the internet. She's got the world at her feet right now – but there's no need to panic.

'Susan is representing Scotland in a huge talent competition. Dropping out would be like Scotland being in the World Cup and saying just before the final, "You know what? I don't think we'll enter." Broadway and Hollywood are possibilities for Susan, but it's one step at a time at the moment. We have to take it a week at a time and if she achieves what I think she can then it's going to be an incredible end for her in *Britain's Got Talent*. That opportunity shouldn't be taken away from her now.

I would love to sit her down for five minutes and say, "Susan, you proved a point, you turned us around in five seconds, I apologise we ever doubted you. We are supporting you, we want you to do well and we're going to be there for you."

'Susan, without any advice from us, won everybody over and I don't want to dictate to her what she should do and what she shouldn't do. What I would say to her is that it's Susan Boyle as a person and as a singer that's more important to me, not whether she has grey hair or brown hair.

'Literally everywhere I go, whether I walk into a shop or a gas station, people come up to me and the first thing they say is Susan Boyle. It's incredible. They love her. People tell me they have watched the clip 50 times and every time it makes them cry.' He added: 'Right now she is one of the most famous people in the world. If nothing else happens, she has acceptance and, for whatever reason, I don't think she had that before.'

By mid-May excitement was mounting as the announcement of the 40 acts that were to make it through to the *BGT* semi-finals drew near.

Susan, carrying a briefcase and wearing a smart blouse, a bright red anorak, and a fluffy pink scarf, took her first flight in eight years when she flew to Heathrow from Scotland to receive voice lessons. She had on a pair of jeans which, fortunately, were done up – Susan had been spotted out and about in a pair with the flies undone a few days before. Her trip to London came because she was one of a number of acts from the programme that were receiving training in advance of the live stages of the show.

Tickets also went on sale for the *BGT* tour of 2009, although none of the artists on the tour had yet been named; it was all dependent on which ten acts made it through to the final.

Perhaps Susan – who now had a permanent bodyguard/minder, whiled away the time on the flight reading a report in one Sunday newspaper linking her with a 66-year-old widower. It was hardly the type of relationship that could be described as 'torrid', however, as the man in question, Helmut Glaser, was quoted as saying, 'Susan had a crush on me last year. We met two years ago at a church group. We met up at prayer meetings for the Legion Of Mary. Susan's lovely – but I'm just too old for her.'

'Then Susan called me last week and asked if I would go to Rome with her to see the Holy Father if she lands a record deal. But I lost my wife in 1988 and I'm too old to get involved with anyone,' added Mr. Glaser, like Susan a devout Catholic. German-born Mr Glaser, who was recovering from an operation, also said, 'I've spoken to Susan on the phone a few times in recent weeks since I got out of hospital. I can only say good things about Susan – when it comes to the crunch she is someone you can rely on. When Susan sings she sings from the heart and I believe she has a gift from God.

'She has always had something special and she's shown that to the world now. I wish her all the best and hope she wins the show. If anyone deserves a little success it's Susan. After what she's been through in life, it shows that God moves in mysterious ways.'

The approaching semi-finals were, in fact, something of a misnomer. There should, to be technically correct, only have been two of them, not the five that were to be transmitted during the week, every one with eight contestants in. But as those nightly eight would be whittled down to a total of ten finalists, 'semi-finals' they were named. The first of these 'semis' would be on Sunday and they would be on every night of the week – barring Wednesday, when there was a massive European football match – before the ten survivors appeared the following Saturday.

Although she was already a favourite to win the show, Susan admitted, 'I have been in my own little bubble getting on with day-to-day life, so I'm not fully aware of what is going on. People tell me about the coverage I am getting from all over the world, but the weirdest thing was when I had a gentleman turn up on my doorstep all the way from Peru. He said he'd seen my clip on YouTube and had come to congratulate me!'

She pledged that there would be no drastic change to her appearance, either. 'I think I am OK. Before the show my looks were not something I ever thought about. We have all entered the show knowing we could win a slot on the Royal Variety in front of Her Majesty, but I honestly think it would be the first time in my life I'd be speechless. I've been practising my song all the time,' she said. 'As for what I am going to wear, that's a surprise."

If the world was agog to see what would happen next to Susan, nowhere was the interest greater than in Blackburn. The Blackburn Community Centre was to be decked out in banners, Scotland flags and bunting and friends were all set to wear special T-shirts.

Organiser Alison Kerr, 49, said: 'I decided to call it a Support Our Susan party and we want to give her the biggest backing we can. We don't know how many people we are going to get on Sunday. We can cater for about 150, possibly rising to 250 if we are deluged. We've got a TV hooked up to a projector and then onto a big screen and we've got digital sound equipment from the centre too. It's all been laid on free by them and it's a fantastic gesture.'

Alison said that if Susan reached the final a bigger venue would be hired. Community centre caretaker Cathy Bryce, said 'I've known her for 20 years, since she first got up to sing at one of the Fauldhouse Miners Club nights. She did a John Cleese silly walk as she made her way to the stage wearing a bright-red Marilyn Monroe-style dress. After she finished "Over The Rainbow", she lifted the dress up over her head.

'Since then we've seen lots of that. She's an eccentric who loves attention. Yet I don't think she realises what she's getting into. Nor do I think she will be able to cope. She's a lovely girl, but she'll have tantrums if things don't go as expected.

'Who knows how she will react if she goes on to win this competition? She's had a very protected life here in Bathgate. If she's successful we'll have another event next week in the big hall which holds 500 people. The town will really want to get behind her.'

At The Happy Valley Hotel – where the car park had been continually filled with TV crews since Susan's first appearance – the bar was festooned with a huge banner, reading 'Good Luck Susan', while posters and newspaper clippings covered the walls.

Manager Jackie Mitchell said, 'We've never had anything like this before. We've just had a couple from Canada who were on holiday and took a detour on the way to the airport to come here. We've had a man from the *Washington Post* and people from Poland and

Croatia. Susan takes it all in her stride. She doesn't seem fussed by it. She's a lovely girl and very down to earth.'

'She wanted the attention for people to stop judging her by her looks. I think she's achieved that. Susan's had a hard life and now she's famous – and she's delighted. I don't think it really matters whether or not she wins, she'll take it all in her stride. I think she'll be okay. She won't get too affected. It's fantastic for the town and it's fantastic for Susan.'

Bartender Kellie Brown was walking to Susan's home several days every week delivering the fan mail that had arrived at the pub.

'Someone from Peru wrote a song for her. There's been mail from all over the world,' she said. Local John Purdon said, 'Everyone's happy for Susan. When she went on we already knew she could sing, but we were surprised by how sassy she was. This is only a wee town, but we've never had anything like this before. She's bigger than the Beatles. This never happened to them. A few days ago some folks from Croatia stopped her in the street and asked for her autograph. But she still comes in here and nobody treats her any different.'

'People come here and want to see her house,' added Sid Mason, another local man. 'I was surprised by the response the world has given her. Most people didn't know where Blackburn was before. If anyone asked you'd say you came from near Bathgate. They know where Blackburn is now.'

Susan's neighbour, Teresa Miller, had given countless doorstep interviews in the five weeks of Susan's fame, and had appeared on television programmes across the Continent. 'It's calmed down now,' she reflected. 'At first you couldn't look out of your window without seeing film crews. If you answered the door to one, there would be ten rushing up to talk to you. Susan couldn't walk out to the shops without them following her. I think Susan's enjoying it. She's on cloud nine. She definitely deserves it. She found it pretty hard when she lost her mum, and the kids used to make a fool of her. We used to hear her singing through the walls. My mum said she was fantastic. I don't think she had the chance years ago. She'd like to make some changes to the house. But she's lived here all her life and I don't think she'll move away.'

Friend Kathleen Stein said, 'Susan knows what she's doing. She has a mind of her own. She didn't even tell us she'd gone to Glasgow for the auditions. She just walked in one day saying she'd made it through. Susan is determined and has real character. Win or lose, she'll carry on singing.'

The Times summed it up on the eve of the announcement of the 40 who would progress into the semi-finals, announcing: 'Unlikely singing star has the whole world in suspense; Susan Boyle is a global sensation, but will she win?

'A fifth of Britain's population are expected to switch on their televisions this evening to watch a dancing dog, a break-dancing pensioner and a man who can do unspeakable things with a clothes hanger. What they and millions around the world will be waiting for, however, is the return of a doughty Scottish lady whose name is known from West Lothian to New South Wales.

'Tonight the world will learn whether she is also considered good enough to proceed to the next round of *Britain's Got Talent*. Assuming that she is, Ms Boyle will perform next week in one of five semi-finals in advance of the final on Saturday evening.

'The shows producers were insisting yesterday that the result of the judges' deliberations be kept secret – a policy that was threatened only when photographs of semi-finalists were apparently posted on the show's website earlier this week.

'Maintaining suspense in the talent contest could prove problematic as the bookmakers appear to regard the result as a foregone conclusion. William Hill placed her as evens to win the contest, and Ladbrokes offered odds of 4-5.'

The Times even quoted Colin Chambers, a professor of drama at Kingston University, saying that the structure of the audition was similar to that of 19th-century melodrama. 'But the story is over. It is quite complete in itself. They have the problem: how do you top that?'

Her appearance was also a problem, he reckoned. 'If she becomes Elaine Paige it would be horrible. If she is seen to have changed in any way I suspect that people would be upset. People warmed to her because she was like anyone else.'

It was no exaggeration to say that the world was waiting on tenterhooks to see what would happen next to Susan. It was inconceivable, surely, that she would not progress to the next stage. Why, wasn't she going to win the eventual title too?

Sure enough she was one of the 40 who were selected, and the news was flashed around the world by various news agencies more accustomed to recording the great disasters and momentous politic events her than sending out an up-to-date on what Melvyn Bragg had remarked, was a talent show after all.

The Press Association said: 'Scottish singing sensation Susan Boyle has made it through to the semi-finals of *Britain's Got Talent* where she will battle it out with 39 other acts. The 48-year-old spinster has gathered a worldwide following and celebrity fans including Demi Moore and Jon Bon Jovi since belting out 'I Dreamed A Dream' from *Les Misérables* on the programme. In a 90-minute special edition of *Britain's Got Talent* on ITV the judges announced the 40 acts they want to go through to the live semi-finals which start on Sunday.

'Two acts from each of the next five shows will be picked by the public and the judges to make it through to the grand final next Saturday. They are all competing for the chance to perform at the Royal Variety Show and a £100,000 cheque.

'Boyle is not the only singer who has captured the judge's attention – a host of cherubic youngsters have also made it through to the semi-finals… The remaining acts from the shortlist of 40 will each perform in front of the judges and the nation over the next week in a bid to win a place in the final.'

Agence France-Presse announced: 'Susan Boyle, the dowdy Scottish spinster whose mighty singing voice has catapulted her to global fame thanks to YouTube, won through to the next round of talent show *Britain's Got Talent* Saturday. A clip of Boyle, 47, in the show's auditions has been watched some 60 million times on the video-sharing website since April and her fans include actress Demi Moore.

As the *Britain's Got Talent* auditions round ended Saturday, Boyle was named among 40 acts who will go through to the live semi-finals from Sunday, when she will make her eagerly-awaited second appearance on the show.

'When asked how she felt after the judges made their decision, Boyle said: "On top of the world, it's fantastic", punched the air and did a dance. Speaking of the semi-finals, she added: "I really want to do my best, get out there and do my best, and anything can happen."

'The grand finale takes place on Saturday May 30 and Boyle – nicknamed the "Hairy Angel" by the British press – is the bookmakers' hot favourite to win…'

The *New York Daily News* trumpeted: 'Susan Boyle – the United Kingdom's biggest singing export since the

Spice Girls – is going through to the next round of *Britain's Got Talent*.'

Susan's reaction was typical: 'I can't believe I'm in the semi-finals,' she said. 'The number of hits on YouTube has just been amazing. Until six weeks ago the only tube I knew of was a tube of Smarties. And the messages of support from all over the world have just been unbelievable and very touching. I never even thought I'd get past the judges. I can't believe I'm in the semi-finals and I've been overwhelmed by the public reaction to my first audition. I'd just like to thank all my fans for the support they have shown me, especially everyone back at home in Bathgate.

'I have got a nice outfit to wear that I'm really happy with, but I just want people to see me for who I am. I'm very nervous and I really don't know what to expect, but I'm just going to go out there and do my best.

'If I get through, bloody fantastic! But I am not thinking that far ahead, just concentrating on my performance. I just want people to see me for who I am, and do my best at singing the song, that's what I am focusing on,' she said.

As her selection was announced she stood in front of the judges in the same dress that had brought titters from the crowd at the Glasgow audition. And when she was given the good news she shook Simon Cowell's hand before doing a little jig of delight in front of Ant and Dec before embracing them both.

There were words of warning, nonetheless, and some of them came from one of the judges. Amanda Holden said, even as Susan was being chosen to progress, 'She'll be an instant international superstar – but I don't think she'll have longevity. I keep thinking, "Thank God we put her through!" We might not have. There were so many brilliant people who didn't make it. She could nail it or kill it. She might not be as good as she was that first night and people put that performance on a pedestal. We've built her up and the public could go, "She's too big for her boots, she's too cocky." She isn't. But we don't like too much success. It's a shame.

'Whether she wins or not, I am sure she's going to have a record contract with Simon and go on to greater things. But this world is fickle. We pick people up and spit them out just as quick. We move on very fast. But who cares? She won't. This is more than she ever dreamed of.'

She also dismissed the rumours that Susan's appearance on the show had somehow been fixed, insisting she'd no idea she'd turn into such a big star. 'To be honest I forgot about her! My husband clearly remembers me coming home from Glasgow and saying, "Oh my God! We found a female Paul Potts, but she's even better." But after that I never mentioned her again. I couldn't believe the controversy about her being a conspiracy. We were hoping for gold and we found it.'

Susan wasn't the only contestant who progressed, of

course, and 39 other acts stood in the way of her winning the contest. Perhaps it's worth recording who they are at this stage. Some might go on to achieve fame, many others instantly became obscure; that's the nature of the beast. But no one could say that weekend in May, what their exact fates would be.

There they all were: Susan, drag artists, wheelbarrow dancers, human saxophones, street artists and several dance groups – including a Greek parody act of Irish folk dancing!

Susan had to take them all on in order to win. Now the public were about to see her live. There were a number of questions that were not yet answered. What would she sing?

And what would she look like?

CHAPTER EIGHT
SuBo Mania

Ant and Dec were dressed to the nines. And so they should have been – it was a special night: the first evening of the semi-finals of *Britain's Got Talent*.

Ant looked at the cameras and said, 'The final act of the night has come all the way from West Lothian in Scotland.' The cheering had already started from among the studio audience before he managed to finish even that brief sentence.

Dec continued the dialogue. 'She is the woman from a tiny village with a big, big voice. I think you know who I am talking about. It's Susan Boyle!'

It was the night of 24 May and Susan was about to give the watching world its second glimpse of her talent. Even Simon Cowell had to admit to the millions glued to their sets, 'The whole world is watching Susan Boyle perform tonight. I would not want to be standing where she is right now.'

A brief reprise of her first appearance was followed by some moody shots of Susan looking out over the countryside and a scattering of words from her. 'In my life I have striven to prove myself, that I can be accepted, that I am not the worthless person people think I am. I have got something to offer,' she said.

Then it was back to Dec who, with a sweep of his arm, said, 'Here she is, please welcome Susan Boyle…!'

In the days running up to that Saturday night on ITV the world had been going 'SuBo' crazy. Every bit of tittle-tattle, every quote, every comment from Susan or the judges, all the background information from Blackburn had all helped to fire the public's imagination.

Would SuBo eventually win? Could anyone stop her? Would Demi Moore fly over for the final? Question after question was being asked by a hungry media on behalf of a voracious public.

Susan was competing against seven other acts that night for two places in the following Saturday's final, and her rivals included dance act Diversity, violinist Sue Son, street performer Nick Hell and ten-year-old singer Natalie Okri, who had been dubbed 'baby Beyonce'. Another of the contestants that evening was Darth Jackson, the Darth Vader/Michael Jackson impersonator.

Susan was rehearsing wearing the 'lucky' dress she had worn for that Glasgow show and she had admitted in the run-up to the evening to feeling 'very nervous' ahead of her first live television performance.

'I never even thought I'd get past the judges. I can't believe I am in the semi-finals and I've been overwhelmed by the public reaction to my first audition. I don't really know what to expect, but I am just going to go out there and do my best again and hopefully the audience and the judges will like my performance. The ultimate dream for me would be to become a professional singer. Meeting Her Majesty the Queen would be the special icing on the cake as she is very regal and is Britain's hallmark.

'If I won I would have a nice holiday, then I would share the money with my family, who have been so supportive and caring,' she said.

After that devastating debut, many people would assume that Susan needed no further help with her voice. But that wasn't the case, and Yvie, the *BGT* voice coach – who in the past had worked with Simon Cowell protégés Leona Lewis and Alexandra Burke – had been assisting her.

'She has a God-given incredible raw talent and a passion that is second to none. I have worked with hugely gifted artists, but when it comes to Susan's genre of music, she is the best I have ever had the pleasure of coaching.

'She will have the whole nation in tears in the live semi-finals. I'll be crying, too. This year there are five or six performers in with a chance of going all the way. No one should underestimate the kids – they are definitely the ones to watch. There is a realness and charm about

Susan that you cannot help but love. She's a normal woman from a wee village in Scotland who happens to have a stunning voice. I was in America when the show first aired. I was watching the news and the presenter started talking about someone on "British Idol".'

She described how she'd watched in awe when Susan sang. 'No matter whether she wins or not, I can't see her jumping into a limo or living a celebrity lifestyle. She was having a right laugh about her mention on *The Simpsons* and I think it's her fantastic sense of humour that will help carry her through all the hype.

'She will have on a new frock and have her hair and make-up done, but that will be it. She will be polished up a bit but not transformed. Like Paul Potts, Susan is pure voice. There is no dressing up or special effects.'

Yvie, who was coaching all the semi-finalists, added, 'I want them all to do well – but of course I would be delighted if we got the first Scottish winner on the show. Whether Susan wins or not she will always be happy as long as she is singing.'

Susan's entrance after the introduction from Ant and Dec could not have been more different from the nondescript stomp-cum-shuffle of her Glasgow audition: dry ice billowed across the stage as the elegantly dressed Susan – in a bronze dress by the show's designer, Stephen Adnitt, and lit by a spotlight high above and behind her, stepped forward. Behind her was a constantly moving image of dark blue clouds, lending an almost ethereal feel to the occasion. Her face seemed a picture of concentration and nerves as she walked towards the microphone, but she managed a smile as she neared it. The song she began to sing was Andrew Lloyd Webber's 'Memory', from *Cats*. What those at the show and watching at home didn't realise was that Susan had been suffering from a cold in the run-up to the evening, so, unlike Glasgow, where she had been sensational from practically the first syllable, she struggled slightly at the start of the song.

Nevertheless her voice, composure and power seemed to grow by the second as she worked her way through the number, finishing to cheers of support.

By the time Ant and Dec had come on stage to talk to her, she was as relaxed as she could be, telling them she felt 'fantastic' and the week had been 'unbelievable'. Had she felt under pressure? 'What pressure?' was her quick reply, adding, 'I have enjoyed every minute of it. I would do it again.'

She blew a kiss to Piers Morgan when he told her she looked beautiful, and he then added, 'I think you were absolutely brilliant. When the world was going through a pretty tough time and we were looking for a bit of inspiration, along came Susan Boyle. On behalf of the whole world – thank you, Susan.'

As the audience clapped loudly Susan gestured beneficently towards them, causing Amanda Holden to quip, 'Susan, you're turning into Eva Peron.'

'I am just so relieved that it went so fantastically well for you,' the actress added. 'I've been biting all my acrylic nails off, and you nailed that performance. I am so proud of you... I am proud you represent Britain so brilliantly... So, well done, thank you.'

And then it was Simon's turn. 'Susan, you're one special lady, I have to say...you really are. And you know what – I just want to apologise for...the way we treated you before you sang the first time. You made me and everyone else look very stupid.'

Susan cheekily shrugged and joked, 'I know nothing. I am from Barcelona', before exiting stage left with all the assurance of a seasoned professional.

As well as the cold she was suffering from, Susan had hardly slept the Saturday before her appearance. 'I'm very nervous. I don't really know what to expect. I'm just going to go out there and do my best again. I haven't had a dramatic transformation. I just want people to see me for who I am and do my best at singing,' she confided.

Of course, she was voted through to the final (how could anything else have happened?) although one or two of the reviewers couldn't resist having little digs at her. One said she had turned into 'more Hollywood than Hairy Monster' while another cuttingly remarked: 'It's an interesting makeover they've given Susan Boyle. Someone's cleaned half her teeth, dressed her in a new frock and teased her hair up into a novelty gonk's quiff, so she now looks like a pop star. Albeit, Micky Dolenz.

They overlooked one crucial thing, however. Her voice isn't actually that great. "Miiiii-dnight?" Only if it's chucking out time at Glasgow's Horse Shoe bar. "Not a sound from the pavement?" You wish, luv.'

The demand from across the Atlantic to watch her sing – President's wife Michelle Obama was said to be desperate to see her again – meant ITV had arranged for it to be streamed onto the internet within minutes of it appearing on television. British theme pubs in the States were arranging SuBo parties so that customers could watch her on widescreen while they downed their drinks.

The public voted Susan into the finals, and dance group Diversity and ten-year-old Natalie Okri received the next biggest share of the public vote and had to face the judges' decision. Amanda Holden threw her weight behind Natalie, but Simon Cowell and Piers Morgan voted for the dancers.

More than 200 people watched Susan sing her way to the finals from the community centre in Blackburn and local councillor Alison Kerr, who organised the event, said the hall erupted in 'pandemonium' as soon as she appeared on screen. 'The atmosphere was absolutely electric, really fantastic,' she said.

'She was so confident tonight and her voice was absolutely wonderful. The minute she was announced the place went into complete pandemonium; it was incredible. As soon as she started to sing everyone went quiet, though – she sounded so fantastic.'

Supporters had decked the hall out in banners and bunting to help create a party atmosphere at the hall where Susan's performance was shown on a big screen.

Mrs Kerr said, 'The hall looks fantastic, all decked out in St Andrew's flag bunting and posters. We were optimistic that she was going to get this far. It's been all hands on deck. This is the biggest party Blackburn has ever seen – heaven knows what the town will be like for the final. Susan has done the whole town proud and there was not a single soul who wasn't watching the telly.'

Kerr – who was at the party with daughter Andrea, 17, and pal Stephanie Nicol, 18 – added, 'The place was a ghost town. If they weren't at our party they were at home in front of the TV.'

Next-door neighbour Teresa Miller, 36, said, 'We hear her singing all the time through the wall. No matter what happens on the show now she is going to be a star all over the world. It's weird to think people will be paying fortunes to see her perform now yet we can hear her all the time. It's wonderful for Susan – she deserves her success.'

Nursery nurse Michelle McCabe, who also lived nearby, had a poster up supporting Susan. 'We got our window decorated yesterday and buzzing is not the word. She asked me to look after her cat Pebbles when she went to the audition in Glasgow but that seemed ages ago and we can hardly believe what's happened. We were watching it on a big telly in the house with a bottle of bubbly ready.'

Friend Jackie Russell added, 'Susan was lonely before this happened to her. Everyone needs a cuddle and she doesn't have that. She goes home alone at night to her cat, but she's got friends and good neighbours and good family. I'm sure there will be male gold-diggers after her now, but she's no fool. She's not as stupid as people are making out.'

Even Scotland's first minister Alex Salmond commented, saying, 'She has Scotland behind her. I'm sure she's got what it takes to be a winner in next week's final.'

Bookmaker William Hill cut her odds of winning to 8/13, the shortest price in the show's history. But if the bookies reckoned she was almost home and dry, not all of her fellow contestants did. Finalist Shaun Smith said that he did not think she was a certainty to win the competition. The 17-year-old singer said he thought all the contestants had a chance of winning. 'Everyone has a chance, every act is absolutely amazing, no one can second guess this competition because anything can happen. Any of tonight's acts, such as Stavros Flatley, could come out and give the performance of their lives and all of sudden they could be the favourites,' he said.

Asked who he thought posed the biggest competition to him, Shaun said, 'Everyone. It's such a level playing field, everyone is so talented it's unreal', although he did admit to admiring Susan's singing. 'I think she's absolutely amazing, her voice is astonishing,' he said.

'The whole point of the show is to give people a shot at something. I would not have had this opportunity if it wasn't for *Britain's Got Talent*. I'd still be a 17-year-old sitting his biology exam absolutely bricking it... You've got all these normal people who need a break and they're finally getting one; that's the best thing about it.'

The 14 million people who tuned in to see Susan meant ITV had an audience share of 54 per cent that evening, proof of the show's popularity.

In an interview with Susan posted on the ITV website, she said: 'I'm feeling really good because it was a totally unexpected result.' She said she had overcome an uncertain start to her performance. 'It was a fairly rocky start to begin with, because to begin with I sort of had a croaky note, but that was because I had a cold. I said to myself, "Well, you'd better just pick yourself up and keep going." So all I did was just keep going and after that it just got better. The audience reaction was really stunning.'

The show was 'completely different' from her audition, she said, adding, 'The pressure was really on me, but you tend to ignore the fact that other people are watching and just concentrate on what's happening in the here and now in that particular studio.'

Not everyone, however, seemed to be in the grip of SuBo mania. Singer Lily Allen, for one. She said on Twitter that 12-year-old Shaheen Jafargholi was more talented than Susan.

The 24-year-old pop singer wrote on her Twitter feed: 'I thought that Susan Boyle's timing was off on *Britain's Got Talent* on Sunday – no control, and I don't think she has an amazing voice. She can sing, Michael Bublé, but it is not about real talent with her, is it? She seems like a lovely lady, but if the show is about talent then that Shaheen kid should win.'

She also said: 'I think *Britain's Got Talent* is verging on child cruelty. That poor little Natalie girl.'

She stood by her views the next day when she 'Tweeted', 'It seems I am not alone. I'd say 90 per cent of you are agreeing with me. And by the way, overrated is not the same as bad.'

The young singer wasn't the only one who had critical views on Susan. *Strictly Come Dancing* Judge Craig Revel Horwood was quoted as saying she was a 'freak of nature'. The choreographer even said she 'sings as bad as she looks'. At the opening night of dance show *Latin Fever* in the West End, Revel Horwood said, 'I think Susan Boyle sucks and I'll tell you why – she can't sing and that really bugs me. I saw her singing "Memory" and she absolutely mauled it. If Elaine Paige or Andrew Lloyd Webber had seen that performance, if they were dead, they'd be spinning in their graves. It was awful. It had major pitch problems throughout. I could go on and on. And that panel of judges just sits there and says how wonderful she was. I was beside myself. I was wanting to smash the TV. I'm hoping people with talent will win, not just the freaks of nature who come out with a little bit of a warble and everyone goes, "Wow!"'

Such comments can hardly have helped Susan, but now that the hurdle of that semi-final was over, there was a great deal worse to come in an astonishing week. The first signs that all was not going to be plain sailing came with reports of her keeping guests awake at the Wembley Plaza Hotel where the contestants were staying – at two o'clock in the morning.

She hardly ever stopped practising, and even in the wee small hours her voice could be clearly heard coming from her room. One guest said, 'She is obviously desperate to win. She just sings all day and all night. It's been keeping me up – it's such a cacophony.' The day after her semi-final triumph she came down into the main area of the hotel and surprised onlookers with her by-now famous shimmy.

She was modest in her assessment of her performance. 'The pressure was really on me. But you tend to ignore the fact that other people are watching. You just concentrate on what's happening in the here and now in that particular studio… Anything can happen – but I'm going to do the really best I can. I just want to thank the people of Britain for getting behind me. You've made my dreams come true.'

But afterwards, she made a somewhat awkward appearance on ITV2's *Britain's Got More Talent*, where she seemed nervous and uncomfortable. Some of her answers to questions barely made sense. At one point she was shown a doll of herself that was for sale. When asked what she thought of it, she put the doll next to her nose instead of giving an answer.

The debate about what song she should sing in the final – Rogers and Hammerstein's 'If I Loved You' and the anthem 'You'll Never Walk Alone' were mentioned as possible candidates – continued, but there was more controversy to come. First, there was the bizarre report that she had donned a Scunthorpe FC shirt for fans and then urged them to sell it on eBay.

Some days later she was widely reported to have reacted in a bizarre manner when hearing Piers Morgan's praise of Shaheen Jafargholi – who was subsequently to reach the final on the judges' votes. Morgan said, 'I think that, pound for pound, that was the best singing performance we've seen so far.' Shaheen's rendition of 'And I Am Telling You I'm Not Going' prompted Morgan to describe it as 'breathtaking'.

Susan apparently reacted in fury to Morgan's praise of the schoolboy and was reported to have stuck two fingers up at a television, shouting 'f*** off' in front of 150 surprised guests before stomping off to her room for the rest of the night.

One witness was quoted as saying, 'Susan was sitting there quite happily with her drink at first. She got a bit annoyed when a busload of tourists asked for autographs and told them to wait until Shaheen had finished. She was smiling as Shaheen sang but afterwards, when Piers started praising him, Susan went nuts.

'She got up, did one of those strange wiggling dances that she does, and then stuck two fingers up at the TV. Then she marched off. We didn't see her again.

'Everyone staying at the hotel gets on really well – it's like one big happy *BGT* family – so everyone was shocked by her outburst.'

A spokeswoman for the show confirmed that Susan had left the bar before the end of the show but added, 'As far as we are aware Susan was not at the bar during Shaheen's performance. She started watching the show there but left early and watched some of the acts in her room because she was being asked for interviews in the bar by journalists.'

There was more to come, and again rumours circulated with different versions of what happened. Under the headline 'SuBo Goes Loco; Exclusive: Temper Boyles Over... Twice', the *Sun* reported: 'She stunned *Britain's Got Talent* fans, contestants and their families before going into meltdown later in front of hundreds of hotel guests. There were fears last night that the pressure was getting to the show favourite. Cops intervened at 5pm yesterday after Susan, 48, went berserk in the lobby of the Wembley Plaza Hotel in North London when two strangers set out to "wind her up". The Scottish singer was heard to roar: "How f***ing dare you! You can't f***ing talk to me like that."

'One of two cops stationed at the hotel went up and asked: "Is there a problem?" Susan, dubbed SuBo, roared: "Of course there's a f***ing problem." Tears flowing, she turned on her heel and marched out the exit followed by her family, production staff and the cops.'

The paper went on to quote an onlooker as saying: 'It took her a long time to calm down from whatever upset her. She was breathing heavily and in a terrible rage. The pressure is obviously getting to Susan. Perhaps all the fame is too much for her.'

A representative of *BGT* offered a different perspective, however, saying that the strangers (later said to be journalists) had been 'trying to wind her up'. He added, 'The police were not called. They were already present.' The entire incident lasted a quarter of an hour. A spokeswoman was quoted as saying, 'Two journalists were harassing her and pushed her over the edge. She was left slightly distressed and the journalists were removed from the building by police.'

Nevertheless, her behaviour prompted the newspaper to report that some neighbours in Blackburn had been known to refer to her as 'Rambo' after the vengeful Sylvester Stallone character in the violent action movies. 'The reason is because if Susan doesn't get what she wants, she goes wild.' Another added, 'It's not unusual to see her freak out over the smallest thing. A few of us think it's only a matter of time before she loses it on the show.'

Something had to be done; the danger signs were there for many to see. Susan Boyle, the biggest 'star' ever on *Britain's Got Talent*, was on the point of quitting the show.

So, two days before the final, Susan was taken from the hotel to a secret hideout in order to escape the intense pressure of the public spotlight she was now in. This was what her success had brought to her life – she'd gone from council house to safe house.

An insider said, 'Show bosses told us to get Susan's mind right because there are genuine concerns about her health. She desperately needs breathing space. The idea is to get into a place where her privacy is better managed than at a hotel. She'll be totally shielded from people other than her closest advisors.'

Writing on his blog, Piers Morgan said, 'Susan is finding it very, very difficult to cope, and to stay calm. She has been in tears many times during the last few days, and even felt like quitting altogether and fleeing all the attention.'

He added, 'Susan Boyle is a very kind, generous-hearted lady who has had a pretty tough life. She was deprived of oxygen during her birth, and that left her with "learning difficulties", causing her to be called "Simple Susan" at school. But she's always, according to people who knew her well, been a fun-loving woman who would do anything to help others. I'm not saying she's a saint. But I am saying that before all this fuss, Susan was generally considered to be a genuinely lovely person – albeit, one with a lively, feisty character, and a wonderfully eccentric sense of humour.'

He said that reading bitchy comments about her had

made him feel 'very, very angry'. 'She's had to read stories and columns, and listen to radio and TV phone-ins, calling her arrogant, insincere, spoiled, fake, mad and so on. Now, I have been called all that and worse in my career, but I spent 20 years in Fleet Street and know how to deal with it. Susan Boyle has never experienced anything like this and is like a frightened rabbit in headlights.'

In a radio interview, Morgan added, 'You could see the nerves almost crippling her on the semi-final show, and I just think it's time that everyone slightly backed off,' adding that she had been 'incredibly upset this week. She's been in floods of tears.'

Morgan was even interviewed by ITN about the state of Susan's mind. 'On Wednesday she was actually going to leave the show, packed her bags to go, because she couldn't see the point in going on if all she was going to get was all this sniping,' he said. 'I think there's a lot of cynicism now building up about Susan, a lot of unnecessary criticism about her and we should give her a break. She's two days away from the biggest show of her life, the biggest moment of her life... She is beginning to realise that her life will never be the same. But, you know, I feel very, very sorry for her.'

Morgan added that talk of Boyle's hotel outburst had been 'massively exaggerated.'

'She is getting this ferocious attention and my heart does go out to her a bit. She is really upset about all this and apparently she's really upset that she may have offended me. You know what, Susan, all you have to concentrate on now is doing an amazing performance on Saturday. You're the red-hot favourite. There are people who want you to fail. There are people who want to snipe at you, who want to kick you because now suddenly you're so popular. All she has to do is do a great performance.'

Morgan was keen to defend the programme, which was now coming in for some criticism, telling the *Radio Times* that it was the opposite of *Big Brother*, the massively popular reality show. 'Big Brother is about celebrating the talentless. *Britain's Got Talent* is 100 per cent about celebrating talent. It not only provokes genuine debate in a tough time for the country, it's put Britain back on the map as a producer of talent.

'I think that Susan Boyle has come as the antidote to the recession. In one little old lady from Scotland we have the cure to all known financial ills.'

He also spoke out about cynicism over the show's auditions. Morgan assured fans that judges have no contact with acts before they go on stage: 'I can tell you that on *BGT* the moment the acts walk in front of the judges is absolutely pure. We genuinely have no idea what is coming our way.'

Susan's brother John, 59, complained that his sister did not have any of the support and back-up that is given to major celebrities. 'Susan is finding it very difficult at the moment. She has become a global sensation and is finding that she doesn't have any of the protection and support that big stars normally do. She is just a normal woman from a small village in Scotland, who all of a sudden is being forced to cope with this on her own.'

Dr Linda Papadopoulos, who had appeared as an analyst on the reality show *Big Brother*, admitted there was a concern that the experience was damaging the singer. 'Somebody who is unprepared for this type of celebrity will find it hugely difficult to deal with. Part of being a celebrity is trying to control your emotions rather than your emotions controlling you and I don't know how capable she will be of doing that,' she said.

Psychologist Dr Aric Sigman, author of a book about that damaging effect TV has on people's lives, said the changes that someone like Susan was going through might be 'very damaging and very hard to cope with.'

A situation such as the one that Susan was now in, where a routine of relative solitude was suddenly ended, could provide a person with 'a great deal of anxiety' and stress, he said. Dr Sigman pointed out that even established celebrities sometimes crack up from the pressure of show business, despite having been accustomed to it for years. He added, 'So is it very surprising that somebody that is very ill-suited for this kind of fame shows the signs of instability?'

Susan's brother John said, 'She has been constantly hounded by fans for the past seven weeks. Like anyone she has a breaking point – she is only human after all.

'If I were in Simon Cowell's shoes I would tell Susan she wouldn't be allowed on the show unless she got her act together. Celebrities have professional people who insulate them from these stresses, but she hasn't had this protection. The show's producers should have been looking after her more.

'Susan used to get picked on and bullied when she was younger. She never reacted. This is a completely one-off incident and won't affect Susan in the slightest.'

Brother Gerry said Susan seemed to be coping despite the pressure as she prepared for the final, where she was favourite to win. 'Susan is under tremendous strain, but she seems to be coping. She would be inhuman not to be nervous. She realises she's a contestant in an open competition.

'She's slightly bemused that people think it's a Susan Boyle show. Her background teaches her not to think that, although she desperately wants to win and have a career around it.

'We're surprised and very happy she has got this far. This is exactly what Susan has wanted to do since she was a little girl. It's amazing that her dream has become a reality. She didn't imagine it would be on this scale. She has come from complete obscurity. I think in these times of depression, it's wonderful to have a story that makes everyone feel great.'

Speculation over Susan was at such a peak that the

day before the final, a spokesman for the show felt compelled to say, 'There is no truth whatsoever that Susan Boyle is leaving the show.'

It was a good job, as up in Blackburn preparations were underway for the Big Day.

Susan's neighbours on Yule Terrace – where new wooden fencing been erected by the council shortly after her first television appearance – had already strung bunting across the street and were hoping to have a giant TV screen installed in time for a massive street party. At the nearby community centre dozens of friends were getting ready to celebrate long into the night if she could pull off her dream.

Manager Ralph Bell said, 'We are expecting four or five hundred people to turn up and have had to move the party from the smaller hall to the basketball courts and have also had to get a risk assessment done. Hopefully we'll have a homecoming party for her, too.'

The Happy Valley was also gearing up for action. 'We are having a party from 7pm until 1am so we can watch the show and then celebrate afterwards once she has won,' one member of staff confidently predicted.

Shops and houses in Blackburn were pasting her image on their windows or hanging flags and banners saying 'Go Susan' and 'Blackburn's Got Talent'.

The local Ladbrokes betting shop expected it to be a busy day. 'People who don't normally bet will have a go, Susan-mania has really hit and it's great to see spirits so high because little else has happened like this around here,' a member of staff commented.

Letters from around the world had been flooding into the local Post Office. A neighbour collected them for Susan on occasions and once even took delivery of a cake made in SuBo's image.

Two tourists from Philadelphia, who had been visiting Edinburgh, decided to drive to Blackburn and stand outside her home, waiting for a glimpse of Susan. Eventually a neighbour told them she was away, let them in to use the bathroom and made them a cup of tea.'

Provost Tom Kerr said the Boyle phenomenon was good for the area. 'We are delighted by anything that promotes and publicises Blackburn and the West Lothian area worldwide. We always knew we had a lot of talent in the area. If Susan wins, we will be having some sort of civic reception,' he added.

'If she wins…' She was the bookmakers' favourite and, in spite of the somewhat bizarre incidents that week, it looked as though nothing would stop her from winning that £100,000 and singing in front of the Queen. But there were still many twists and turns left in the short, yet eventful, singing life of Susan Boyle.

CHAPTER NINE
REALITY BITES

The bookmakers had Susan as their firm favourite to walk off with the *Britain's Got Talent* title, and bookmakers are not in the habit of making too many mistakcs.

Despite the problems of the week leading up to the final, the outbursts – real, imaginary or exaggerated – the flight to the safe house and the strange behaviour, Susan was still the one to beat in the eyes of the men and women who set the odds.

One supporter from Devon backed her to win to the tune of £7,000. Over £3 million in total was placed on the outcome of the contest – an amazing example of how reality TV betting, which had taken off with the arrival of Big Brother, was now big business.

The FA Cup final 2009 between Chelsea and Everton coincided with the day of the *BGT* final and they were now equal in their importance to the bookmakers.

A spokesman for one of the large bookmakers said, 'Five years ago the idea of a TV programme competing with the FA Cup final would have been laughable, but now we've given them equal space.'

'Big Brother got the ball rolling and that really changed betting in quite a big way,' he said. 'All the reality television that came after that, from your *Pop Idol* to *The X Factor* and now *Britain's Got Talent*, brought in a completely new betting clientele. People who wouldn't have dreamt of putting a bet on the horses or a football match, but reality TV was something they knew about.'

William Hill was offering odds of 10/11 after a surge in betting and a spokesman said, 'We briefly offered Susan Boyle at 11/10 – a price that proved too tempting for punters. As far as we are concerned she just needs to turn up to win this.'

The judges, too, were ultra-supportive. Simon Cowell revealed that he'd had a heart-to-heart with the nervous songbird, assuring her protection against any threat to her health, telling her, 'You've come so far, don't give up on your dream now. I have never known anything like this in my whole career.

'I just wanted to make sure she was OK. I told her I would help her in any way I can. She has earned the right to be in that final and I didn't want her to miss out on her big night.'

Amanda Holden said, 'She will definitely be in the final. She won't let the pressure get to her and she'll do a great job. Hopefully she will sing "I Dreamed A Dream", which is what everybody would love her to do. She's not going to quit. I think she did have her bags packed at one stage, but I think basically that was just because she was feeling so sad and upset.

'You can't train somebody in four weeks to handle this kind of attention. She is under a lot of pressure but no one can blame her – I still think she could win it.'

Piers Morgan was even more up-front. 'My bet is that she will respond with the performance of her life. This is one tough lady who has had to fight since the day she was born, and there is no way she's going to quit now, trust me. Susan's going to be a major star whatever happens. And I hope she nails it on the night, and shoves all these vile critics' disgraceful attacks down their throats.'

Demi Moore, who at one stage had been rumoured to be flying over to see the final, said, 'The whole world is rooting for you whatever the outcome. You have nothing to lose – just keep sharing your light.'

Elaine Paige too was in Susan's corner. 'I'll be watching with my fingers crossed for you,' she said. Even Hillary Clinton, the US Secretary of State and wife of the former President, said Boyle was 'an inspiration' who was admired across America. 'She has risen to fame, with millions of admirers here, all on her amazing talent and a prayer. In these trying times this should be a lesson and a shining example of substance over mere packaging.'

Royalty wasn't immune to the attraction of the show,

either, although not totally in Susan's favour. Prince Harry was on an official visit to New York when he was asked what he thought of Susan. He pulled a face and said, 'Er, actually I really like the saxophone player.'

Susan was probably unaware of what the young prince thought – or of the fact that SuBo Mania had spread to eBay. On the day of the final there were 300-plus items linked, albeit it very vaguely, with her. There was an astonishing range of goods, from mouse mats to key rings, fridge magnets to clocks. Admirers could even buy a replica gold dress similar to the one she first wore at the Glasgow audition.

CDs of Susan singing 'Cry Me a River' during that charity recording were still fetching hundreds of pounds, while a Susan Boyle internet domain name was on the market for £327. There was a Susan Boyle novelty £1 million banknote for £1.27, fridge magnets for £1.99, 'I Love Susan Boyle' T-shirts for £7.99 and a kitchen clock for £3.99. 'I Dreamed A Dream' mugs for £9.35 from the United States, or even a 1934 Musical Powder Puff Box, programmed with her song, for £8.10. Pillowcases (£7.99), Susan Boyle 'Hell Yeah' car number plates (£9.95), a cuddly dog toy with Susan Boyle eyebrows (99p), leather jewellery cases from Malaysia (£9.97) and 'Kiss Me Susan Boyle' T-shirts (£10.99) were among the more unusual items.

There were a number of oil paintings of her too, usually based on her audition. By the morning of the final, 'I Dreamed A Dream' had been watched more than 220 million times on YouTube and the frenzy showed no sign of abating: 'Memory' had already been viewed by 16.8 million people in the five days since it had been broadcast.

Those figures showed how the impact she had made dwarfed the interest shown in her rivals and the odds the bookmakers were quoting also showed how far behind Susan it was thought all the other competitors were in the race for the title.

The strange mixture of young and old who made up the nine other acts who all hoped to defeat the favourite in front of an anticipated audience of 20 million was as follows:

STAVROS FLATLEY: 8/1

Third favourites to win, Demetrios Demetriou, 41, and son Mikalakis, 12, the father-and-son Greek comedy dance act from north London, had built a large fan-base with their spoof dance act.

SHAUN SMITH: 25/1

A handsome, rugby-playing 17-year-old from Lichfield, Staffs, tipped as the dark horse of this year's competition. His rendition of 'Ain't No Sunshine' at his audition was stunning and he swept through to the final with U2's 'With or Without You'.

SHAHEEN JAFARGHOLI: 6/1

The second favourite with his own celebrity fans including Lily Allen, Sir Tom Jones and Beyoncé. The 12-year-old from Wales was seen as the most dangerous rival to Susan.

FLAWLESS: 10/1

Their name says it all. Impeccable timing and choreography had made some viewers believe that this 10-strong dance group of north Londoners could win.

JULIAN SMITH: 12/1

The shy and unassuming self-taught Brummie saxophonist wowed the judges and the audience at his audition and semi-final.

TWO GRAND: 33/1

Grandfather and granddaughter singers John O'Neil, 76, and Sallie Lax, 12, from Doncaster. The duo were so over-sweet in their performance that Simon Cowell likened them to 'having seven sugars in your tea'.

DIVERSITY: 10/1

This 10-strong band of brothers and friends were giving fellow dance troupe Flawless a run for their money.

AIDAN DAVIS: 25/1

The 11-year-old hip-hop dancer, who Simon Cowell said

was 'super, super, super talented', body-popped his way to the final.

HOLLIE STEEL: 25/1

Simon Cowell had called the Lancashire ten-year-old 'the bravest girl in the world'. Hollie burst into tears during her first attempt at singing 'Edelweiss' – after a hug from her mother she was allowed to take to the stage again when she delivered a note-perfect performance.

The excitement was mounting around the world, although Susan's brother, John Boyle, appeared to have his feelings more under control than many.

He travelled almost 400 miles from his home in Blackburn to London for the *BGT* final on Saturday but decided not to attend the final, choosing to visit relatives instead.

'It [the show] can go on for three hours and it can get boring after a while. I travelled to London, but I took the decision not to go to the studio. I went to my niece's house in London to spend the night there,' he revealed. 'It was a deliberate decision on my part. Susan had plenty of people there backing her. I thought it was better to let the youngsters in the family go along instead.'

Whether or not he was present, Susan was apparently revving up for her chance. 'I want nothing more than to stay and sing in the *Britain's Got Talent* final. I've spent weeks rehearsing. It's all I've been thinking about. I'm not going to throw away my big chance now.'

Piers Morgan said she was in 'very good spirits' before the show, in spite of her outburst during the week. 'They have a whole army of doctors, psychiatrists and experts available to any contestant at any time. They have all been taking great care of Susan. Susan Boyle is a very, very nice lady from Scotland who never thought she would have this chance and she is really looking forward to it.'

One of the other finalists, 73-year-old break-dancer Fred Bowers, viewed things slightly differently and was quoted as saying that she alienated fellow contestants. 'We've realised she can be really aggressive. One minute she's laughing and then she turns.'

Others, who had known her longer than Morgan or Bowers, had their own view on Susan and her temperament. Doug Malloy, a bass player who had accompanied her for 20 years, said, 'Susan is a really nice person, but she is highly strung. If you were backing her and you hit a bum note, she would give you this look, one of those that can kill. She will not put up with people talking in the audience when she is singing. She would throw a tantrum right there on stage.'

Arthur Murray, 66, a guitarist and another of her long-time backing musicians, said, 'There is no question about her ability as a singer. When I backed her, she used to do some stuff from the Carpenters, and she also loved musicals, like *Jesus Christ Superstar*. Everybody here knows she is a great singer, but because of her problems, people just don't seem to take her seriously. I always knew she had the talent to make it big, but I would have been worried about her temperament. With Susan, you would never know what to expect. When she was on form, she was unbeatable.'

So, would she be unbeatable that night of 30 May 2009, in front of what turned out to be the largest television audience in Britain since England played Portugal in the 2006 World Cup finals? What those millions at home didn't know was what was going through her head. This is how she later put it:

'With no pressure on top of me and suddenly all this pressure, I found it a bit suffocating. I was feeling very anxious during the final. It got so bad I was actually staring at the walls. I didn't want to know anybody.'

What torment must have been going on inside her at that moment when Ant and Dec introduced her, the eighth act on stage? Yet there she was, standing alone on stage in her elegant blue, full-length dress literally in the spotlight, having to perform again. And she was magnificent.

The nerves of 'Memory' a week earlier were forgotten as she chose to reprise her audition song, 'I Dreamed A Dream'. At times she seemed to be screwing up her face as though looking at some downward, distant object through a mist, as though the doubts of the previous week were sitting like demons on her shoulders. At other moments she shook her head defiantly to the side and back again in some Judy Garland-esque gesture of defiance, a movement that brought a fleeting, almost paternal, smile from Simon Cowell.

Then, the 'ordeal' over, came the questions. Ant said, 'Well done Susan, fantastic reaction, all the judges on their feet. How was that for you? You have had a lot of pressure on you this week, but you went out there and performed and it seemed like you really enjoyed that.' Susan replied, 'I would like to thank people and all the support they have given me, especially the people at home, the people in the audience. I'd like to thank everyone for all their support.'

Dec asked, 'It has been a week with a lot of pressure for all the acts, none more so than you, but was that worth it, in front of everyone here?' 'Well worth it! Well worth everything,' Susan replied.

'That's where you really feel at home isn't it, on stage?' enquired Ant. Susan nodded, saying, 'I really feel at home on stage, of course I do, I am among friends, am I not?'

Then it was the judges' turn to give their verdicts on the woman who had captured the imagination of the world.

Piers Morgan was first: 'Wow, Susan, you've had a very difficult week. You have had an amazing seven weeks, but a very difficult week where you have been the centre of the world's attention. There have been negative headlines, you have been boiling over, cracking up, going to quit the show, all this kind of thing. And quietly all I kept thinking to myself was, all you have to do to answer all your critics, is walk down that stage to that microphone, sing the song that we all fell in love with, sing it better than you did last time.'

At that last remark, Susan rolled her eyes in pleasant surprise.

'Susan,' he continued, 'I'm not supposed to favour anyone as a judge, I should be impartial, but you know what, forget it, that to me was the greatest performance I've seen in *Britain's Got Talent* history. You should win this competition. I loved it.'

At this Susan put her hands to her face, turned around and tapped the back of her head.

Amanda Holden was next: 'Susan, I have never heard such powerful, confident vocals. You absolutely, you sang it so well this evening and I just echo what Piers said really. You, out of everybody this week, have been under an enormous amount of pressure. But you did it girl. You did it for Scotland and you did it for Great Britain. And, can I just say, Simon had a tear in his eye and I've never seen that before.'

Finally came Simon Cowell's judgement: 'Susan, I don't know who's going to win this competition. But you know you have had a weird seven weeks and you had every right to walk away from this.

'You could have had a lot of stuff coming your way in America and a lot of people said you shouldn't even be in this competition, that you are not equipped to deal with it. For what? For you to sit at home with your cat and say, "I've missed an opportunity." I completely disagree with that.'

In the midst of his speech, Susan gently stroked one of her hands with the other.

'And you know, win or lose, you have the guts to come back here tonight, face your critics and you beat them. And that's the most important thing. Whatever happens Susan, I've got to know the real Susan Boyle, which is not the person I've seen portrayed in the media, who is still a very nice, shy person who just wants a break. You can walk away from this with your head held high. Susan. I absolutely adore you.'

The viewers' votes had to be counted and that meant all ten acts stood on stage. Ant and Dec announced the top three: first to be revealed was Susan, followed by Diversity and then came Julian Smith. Everything seemed to be on course. The bookmakers were on the point of losing the £5 million riding on Susan. Third place belonged to Julian Smith, Ant and Dec announced, and after a few words from the soulful saxophonist he walked off stage.

The Geordie hosts stood in between Susan on one side, matronly and tense, and Diversity, all youth and energy, on the other.

Dec solemnly looked at the camera and intoned, 'It has been an amazing final tonight. That's it. One of you is going to win £100,000 and that place on this year's

Royal Variety Performance. Good luck to both of you. The winner of *BGT* 2009 is…'

And then he paused. The youngsters were moving around nervously; Susan seemed to be concentrating even harder than usual and was mouthing thoughts to herself.

A pause for dramatic effect is one thing, but the silence lasted 16 painful seconds before he said to the millions on the edge of their seats '…Diversity.'

The dancers went wild with delight. Susan smiled.

Dec turned to her and said, 'With every competition there has to be a runner-up and this year what a fantastic competitor. Susan, how do you feel right now?'

'The best people won,' was her response, adding, 'They are very entertaining, lads. I wish you all the best.'

Dec said to her, 'That is very gracious. I want to say that on behalf of us all at *Britain's Got Talent*, it has been amazing to meet you and we have all shared an amazing journey with you over the last seven weeks, you have been phenomenal. Let's hear it for the runner-up, Susan Boyle!'

During this warm tribute from the hosts Susan reacted in typical fashion: she did a semi-curtsey, wiggled her hips and arms, did a small dance and finally raised her skirt above the knee to show the world her left thigh.

Diversity were still going crazy. They had every right to. Even Simon Cowell had been fulsome in his praise: 'All bets are off. If I had to give marks on that this would be the only performance tonight that I would give a ten to. I have got to say that when I'm looking at you standing there together, the fact you pulled it all together with not a step out of place, it was sheer and utter perfection.'

And Amanda Holden had told them: 'You have practically rendered me speechless. Ashley [Banjo] your choreography is second to none. The rest of your team follows you to the letter. I think you have blown Flawless [the other street-dance finalists] out of the water. There is definitely room for you out there.'

The waiting world was soon being told the results of the *BGT* final via news bulletins, the internet and newspaper reports. The story wasn't, of course, that Diversity had won. That wasn't the story. The real story, the only one that most people cared about, the information they had been waiting for was the other side of the coin... Susan Boyle had lost!

Susan Boyle, the odds-on favourite; Susan Boyle, the woman the bookies reckoned had it in the bag; Susan Boyle, one of the most famous, instantly recognisable people on the planet, had not won. She had come second. The viewing public who had to decide who would be the winner had chosen someone else. It seemed barely believable. It was not credible.

Hadn't she been on the *Oprah Winfrey* show for goodness sake? And *Larry King*, too? Even her cat Pebbles was a celebrity now. Her West Lothian home town had been visited by more film crews than most frontline battle zones. Stars had Tweeted about her, said they would like to sing duets with her, marvelled at her talent. Surely there had been some mistake?

But there had been no mistake. It seems unkind to Diversity to be anything less than fulsome in praise of them, but many wondered how they could have got more votes than Susan? Perhaps the younger element in the audience had decided Diversity were the ones to choose. Perhaps, just perhaps, the 'cult' of SuBo had acted in a perverse way against Susan. Had the negative remarks and reports in some parts of the media about her treatment and her reaction to fame turned the voting public against her?

Whatever the reason, what had been done was done. She'd lost. Late that night there were some 'after-match' quotes from some of the key players in the drama. Dec admitted he was stunned at the result. 'It's a shock result, which was good for the show. People have been through mixed feelings about Susan. They loved her one minute and the next they went off her. But what people have to remember is we've only seen her sing live three times.'

Ant added, 'That lady has had the most phenomenal seven weeks. It might be a blessing in disguise that she didn't win.'

Simon Cowell's view was, 'Diversity were absolutely incredible. I'm gutted for Susan. She was there at the top all the way through. But she was incredibly gracious. Susan has come out of this very well. We've never had a runner-up like Susan before.

'She won over a lot of fans tonight, not just with her voice, but with her graciousness. She's got a massive future in front of her.'

The *Independent on Sunday* told its readers the next morning: 'Cinderella will not be going to the ball. Susan Boyle, whose singing has transformed her in the past month from a slightly dotty-looking spinster into a worldwide inspiration, last night sensationally lost the final of the show that made her – *Britain's Got Talent*.

'Despite an assured reprise of "I Dreamed a Dream", the song that made her a YouTube phenomenon, she was defeated by the dance troupe Diversity, and so will not get to sing for the Queen, after all. The 10-strong troupe from Essex stood open-mouthed with disbelief as they realised they would leave with a £100,000 cheque and a booking at the Royal Variety Performance. Beside them on the stage, Boyle quivered with nerves. "The best people won", she said, before wishing them "all the best".

'"As far as we are concerned, she just needs to turn up to win this," Rupert Adams, of William Hill, had said hours before the show.

'The disappointment capped a tumultuous six weeks for Boyle... She has found sudden fame hard to deal with, and as tension mounted last week she was said to be struggling to cope.'

The *People* announced: 'Dance troupe Diversity were the shock winners of *Britain's Got Talent* last night – in a shock defeat of favourite Susan Boyle... Diversity group leader Ashley Banjo was stunned by their victory. The choreographer thanked the millions of viewers who voted for them and said: "I was saying, 'Guys, second.' I cannot believe it, I'm going to wake up in a minute."

'Of the four million votes cast, Diversity won 24.9 per cent, SuBo 20.2 per cent and Julian 16.4 per cent.

'Ashley admitted he believed Susan would win. He said: "I honestly think that the amount of media attention that she's had, if someone beat her it would have to be one spectacular performance. She has an amazing story, obviously everyone laughed at her when she came on then she began to sing. She's got an amazing voice and talent. But you never know, I'd like to think we can give her a run for her money."

'It had long been predicted that Susan, from Blackburn, West Lothian, Scotland, would snatch the crown.'

The *News of the World* had reached its own conclusions as to why she failed to win: 'Susan Boyle's shock defeat in the *Britain's Got Talent* final was last night blamed on a last minute SuBo backlash. Millions turned against the spinster, from Blackburn, West Lothian, after a four-letter tirade at fans – and switched votes to surprise 12-1 winners Diversity. Host Declan Donnelly said: "People loved her one minute and next they went off her."'

The *Observer*, the world's oldest Sunday newspaper, was also taken by surprise. 'In the end, Susan Boyle's dream of winning *Britain's Got Talent* remained just that. With bookies offering odds of 10-11 that she would clinch victory over the show's strongest-ever field, last night's climax was supposed to belong to the 48-year-old Scottish spinster who has become a global phenomenon. But when results of the final public vote were announced, Diversity, a youthful 10-member dance group from Essex, had pushed her into second place, in front of a TV audience of up to 20 million.'

The *Sunday Express* confirmed that reaction to the upset was universal: 'Stunned dancers Diversity jumped for joy and embraced each other in emotional scenes as they were named the winners of ITV1's *Britain's Got Talent* last night.

'The dramatic final had millions of viewers teetering on the edge of their sofas – and some may have fallen off at the shock result.

'Bookies greeted the result with relief, as they were set for a £5 million payout if Boyle had taken the title. David Williams of Ladbrokes said: "Susan came unstuck and we're breathing a huge sigh of relief. We were staring down the barrel of a mega payout on her. Diversity have ridden to the rescue of bookies and we'll be sending them a bottle of champers. It was a one-horse race all the way up to the weekend and only became interesting at the last minute."'

Susan's fame had been instant; the global village heard and more importantly saw her arrival on the stage of that Glasgow auditorium in practically the blinking of an eye. The same was now true of her failure.

The *New York Post* said: 'She is an internationally acclaimed Internet phenomenon and a symbol of the folly of underestimating people because of the way they look. But in a shocking upset, Susan Boyle, the 47-year-old Scottish church volunteer whose stunning audition for the *Britain's Got Talent* TV show last month has been viewed something like 90 million times on YouTube, lost in the final round of the program on Saturday night.

'After the audience votes had been tallied, Ms. Boyle was placed second, beaten by a joyfully innovative dance troupe named Diversity.

'Winners of *Britain's Got Talent*, one of a host of talent shows that are among the most-watched programs in Britain, receive about $160,000 and a spot on the roster of the Royal Variety Performance, presented in front of the Queen. Their high profiles also virtually assure that they will have lucrative careers in show business.

'But the same is often true for the runners-up, who in this case included Julian Smith, a soulful saxophonist who was a darling of the studio audience and came in third. And the exposure Ms. Boyle has received since her original audition, culminating in an appearance on *Oprah* in the United States, means she is a hot property who is virtually guaranteed a recording contract.'

The *New York Times* also went big on the sensational result: 'Frumpy singing sensation Susan Boyle lost in a stunning upset yesterday on the British TV talent show where she had become an international Internet sensation last month with her incredible rendition of "I Dreamed a Dream" from *Les Misérables*.

'The UK public picked a dance troupe called Diversity as the winner of *Britain's Got Talent* over the Scottish songbird, who came in second out of a group of 10 finalists.

'Diversity's victory came completely out of left-field, as all signs pointed to victory for Boyle, a lonely, small-town church volunteer who shocked audiences with golden pipes that belied her dowdy appearance. After her defeat, the 48-year-old Boyle curtsied to the audience before delivering her goofy, signature hip shake.'

And in Chicago, the *Tribune* wrote: 'She dreamed a dream, and it very nearly came true. But Susan Boyle's reality show journey ended Saturday with a second-place finish in the finals of *Britain's Got.Talent*, an ending that didn't fit the fairy tale. Instead of the 48-year-old Internet sensation, an exuberant dance troupe called Diversity took the $159,000 prize and will perform for Queen Elizabeth II at the Royal Variety show.

'Boyle paced the stage as the hosts named the top three of the 10 final acts and looked almost relieved when her name was called as the runner-up. She recovered in time to graciously praise the dancers... It had been a tumultuous week for Boyle, a woman previously unused to the limelight. She lost her cool during a confrontation with two reporters, and the police intervened. One contest judge said Boyle had contemplated pulling out of the competition to soothe her frazzled nerves.

'But when she stepped into the spotlight Saturday, Boyle seemed more polished – and animated – than in previous appearances.'

So unexpected was Susan's defeat, it even made headlines in Azerbaijan, the Eastern European country on the Caspian Sea. The story there read: 'Dance group Diversity won the television show *Britain's Got Talent* on Saturday night, upsetting Scottish singer and internet sensation Susan Boyle. "The best people won," Boyle said. The 48-year-old church volunteer had been favoured to win the show. The show winner claims 100,000 British pounds ($161,000) and will perform for Queen Elizabeth II in the Royal Variety Show.'

Seven weeks earlier she had been unknown outside of Blackburn. Now people in a tiny country at the border of Europe and Asia were eager for news of her fate.

Back home there was sympathy for her from many quarters. In Scotland, First Minister Alex Salmond said, 'Over the past couple of months, Susan has wowed the judges and the public with her incredible voice and display of supreme talent, and I'm sure she's got what it takes to go on and have a hugely successful musical career if that's what she decides to do. Scotland is very proud of Susan's incredible singing.'

Blackburn Community Centre manager Ralph Bell said, 'We were disappointed that she lost, but we're still very proud of what she's achieved. You have to be here to appreciate how much feeling there is for her locally and we said at the beginning of the night, it doesn't matter what the result is.'

'She's definitely got a big future,' he added. 'You can tell from her performance tonight that she was terrific and long may that continue.'

Scottish Secretary Jim Murphy revealed he voted for her in every round. 'Tonight's performance was spectacular and her best yet,' he said. 'Susan is a brave and brilliant talent. She bounced back and showed that she is a real star. She has proven all the cynics and critics wrong. Susan has gone from our favourite underdog to a worldwide phenomenon in just seven special weeks.'

There were those, however, who thought that failing to win might actually have been a good thing for Susan. Surprising as it may seem, Piers Morgan was one of them. 'I do think it may turn out to be the best thing that happens to her, coming second. I think she has found a lot of it quite hard to deal with and I think the pressure of actually winning and living up to all that expectation would have just carried on the mayhem for her. I'm only sorry that the extraordinary tidal wave of publicity she attracted meant so many people got either bored or irritated by Boyle mania and decided not to vote for her.'

Speaking 48 hours after the show, he said, 'Nobody has had to put up with the kind of attention Susan has had. Nobody could have predicted it. It has been crazy, she has gone from anonymity to being the most downloaded woman in history.'

He said that the length of time Boyle had to wait between her semi-final performance and the final, a week later, had added to the pressure. 'It just builds and builds and builds.'

Unlike the other contestants, she had been subject to attention from international media and Morgan added that: 'A little bit of negativity crept in. She was very tired and hasn't been sleeping. She has just gone away to have some time to herself and to sleep and eat, doing all the things she hasn't been able to do in the last week. Her dream was not to win a talent competition, it was to sing professionally and she will do that.'

But the disquiet that had existed in some quarters about Susan's success was about to expand and explode. It would be hard to imagine two newspapers more dissimilar than the *Guardian* and the *News of the World*. One an upmarket left-orientated paper for the so-called intelligentsia, the other a mass-market tabloid famous for its blunt and often scandalous views on life and British society. Yet they were both to express similar concern about Susan and her treatment.

Tanya Gold, writing in the *Guardian*, had been one of

the first to question SuBo mania, not as a criticism of Susan but rather as an examination of the nation's fascination with her. Her verdict on the final and the result was damning.

'Susan Boyle didn't win *Britain's Got Talent* on Saturday night because she became the wrong kind of victim. We loved her at first, because she was a pitiful, pathetic, unattractive 48-year-old Scottish virgin who lived with a cat – a strange creature in a dull gold dress, who didn't belong on a stage. And when we heard her singing "I Dreamed a Dream" at her audition we thought: we can change your life. We can make you happy. We can save you. Behold our kindness, Susan Boyle, and weep tears of happiness.

'In *Britain's Got Talent* it is never simply the talent that wins. It is the journey that wins – the story that the British public deems most worthy of reward. Who from the fetid gutter shall we raise up to be a glittering star? Who will be the most appreciative candidate? At first we thought it must be Susan Boyle, who the tabloids nicknamed "the hairy angel". It is a despicable phrase, but it says everything about what we expected Susan Boyle to be. It means "ugly saint".

'But last week Susan Boyle began to step out of her journey. It was reported that she was cracking up under the pressure. The "hairy angel" was becoming aggressive. She wasn't, in fact, an angel, but she was human, and troubled... Susan, we read on, was being counselled by "armies of psychiatrists" as she prepared for the big final on Saturday night. Piers Morgan reported that she had "been in tears repeatedly" and had even packed her bags, ready to walk away from the contest entirely. What's up, Susan Boyle? Don't you feel better after all we have given you? Aren't you grateful?'

She went on to discuss why we were baffled by the anger Susan showed. 'It was like realising that Cinderella didn't have an orgasm on her wedding night – or that Snow White actually hated the dwarves... The deal was – we will save you, but you have to be the kind of victim that we want. You have to be blemish-free and passive and inert. You have to be grateful, and you are not allowed to be confused about it. We will rescue you, Susan Boyle, and you will be rescued. You will exist only for your redemption... We don't really want to think about what we did to Susan Boyle, before she even stepped on to the stage. And to all the other Susan Boyles whom we ignored and neglected and mocked, because they are ordinary women, without breast implants or an overt sexuality or Amanda Holden's curiously joyless face... When Susan Boyle sang "I Dreamed a Dream" she offered us a chance to redeem our guilt. But when we realised that we couldn't save her, and that we couldn't make it all right with a stupid television talent show, we dropped her, right back where we found her.'

Savage stuff from Ms Gold, but Carole Malone in the

News of the World was hardly wearing kid gloves either when she wrote:

'Won? Lost? It doesn't actually matter. What matters is that Susan Boyle is on the road to hell. And I can't be happy for what's happened to her or what's about to happen because I fear it's going to destroy her. I'm terrified that it isn't just her newfound career that's going to fall apart – but her whole life as well.

'Because everyone is still skirting around the problem. Experts are talking about her "psychological problems", about her "fragile mental state", about her "delusional attachment to Piers Morgan".

'No one is actually saying what the REAL problem is. But we all know don't we? And now they're claiming it's the pressure of celebrity that's got to her. It isn't. It's the pressure of her condition. It's the pressure of being taken away from the small Scottish village where she was able to cope with life because it was simple and safe.

'Susan was able to live THAT life because the people around her accepted her "eccentricities" and made allowances for her. And while she wasn't always able to control her temper or her feelings, the locals looked after her because she was one of them.'

And the columnist added: 'And yes, we all got carried away watching life come good for this quirky, chubby, funny-looking little virgin from West Lothian who was always making funny faces, wiggling her hips and giggling that she'd never been kissed.

'But we all knew, didn't we? We could all see. Which is why we're as much to blame for what's happened to Susan Boyle as those TV bosses suddenly feigning horror at her mental state... And no, I don't buy the excuse they were just giving her what she'd always wanted. I'm sorry but, with respect, Susan Boyle isn't capable of knowing what she wants or what the world of celebrity has in store for her. And that's not patronising, it's just recognising who she is – something TV bosses surely would have done a long time ago had they not been blinded by £ signs... There WAS a window there where her story was all sweet and heart-warming and lovely, but it's gone.

'In its place is a fragile, mixed-up woman in crisis who's sobbing and shouting and swearing because she doesn't understand and can't handle what's happening to her. The truth is, we were all knocked sideways by Susan Boyle because as a society we've been conditioned not to expect anything from people like her... But what will become of her now? I expect she'll do a few interviews in the States, maybe even make an album – but I expect that will be it.

'And then what? Back to West Lothian where, thanks to *BGT*, she no longer belongs?'

The broadcaster and writer Libby Purves raised some further, and disturbing, points in *The Times*: 'On Saturday night the shy Scotswoman Susan Boyle sang her last song on the ITV show *Britain's Got Talent*, and didn't quite win. She was beaten by the street-dance group Diversity, and it was probably for the best... Maybe this time, the fame-dragon will be cheated of its human sacrifice, tamed and bridled and taught its place. Susan Boyle can continue to prosper in a lower wattage of spotlight. The most poignant moment of the evening came as she smilingly conceded to the dancers and – pressed for her feelings – looked out at the audience and said: "I'm among friends... am I not?" The last three words cut deep. Those who feed off the apparent love of audiences always hope that they are among friends. But deep down, they doubt it. And there is real danger in a storm of applause and attention: it can wash the soul away unless it is anchored by the solidity of family and friends, who do not clap or adore but merely hug and gently mock... Most will admit to tearful, lonely or drunken times in hotels and dressing-rooms where they wonder if anybody will ever want them again for themselves, not just their public shtick.

'Overdoses of fame can be lethal: they often douse the creative spark and drive the artist into noisy self-parody and consequent self-hate. In a way, the new phenomenon of empty celebrity unbacked by original talent is less destructive: any amount of fame can't do much harm to the oeuvre of Piers Morgan or Paris Hilton.'

As if these scathing critiques were not merciless enough, they seemed tame compared to the *Independent*'s verdict:

'A country that not only tolerates the celebrity of

Simon Cowell and Piers Morgan but considers them as competent arbiters of aesthetic achievement has clearly lost its way. Of course it is part of the gag that these repulsive individuals constitute two-thirds of the judging panel, but it is not a gag that I find particularly amusing, or one that reflects at all well on those of you who endorse it.

'The staggering success of Susan Boyle provides us with a neat encapsulation of all that has gone wrong with Britain. It is not her fault that she considers "I Dreamed A Dream" a suitable vehicle for her talents. Were she to stand up and belt it out at the end of the evening in her West Lothian local, The Happy Valley, it would actually be both hilarious and touching – and even I would raise a glass to her and give her a hand, for sheer brass neck if for nothing else – but for her to become an "international sensation"?

'When did it become mandatory to give pap like this our wholehearted approval? It's not a song; it's an insult to the very idea of songwriting. "I Dreamed A Dream", forsooth. What else are you going to do with a dream, genius? Yes, yes, I know the show is all about popular entertainment. But since when does "popular entertainment" become synonymous with rubbish? But these days it is cheap sentimentality that has triumphed, and all we have now is a culture that has become homogeneous, entirely bland. It's not Susan Boyle's fault. It's ours.'

Susan Boyle – Living the Dream

The controversy about Susan Boyle's treatment by both the television which had given her fame and the public's fascination with her continued, but there was an even larger and more disturbing development ahead.

CHAPTER TEN

FAME & MISFORTUNES

Now that Susan's attempt to win *Britain's Got Talent* had ended, that surely would be that for a while. The storm that had been raging around her would go away, the publicity would diminish, the world would not be quite so interested any more. She could 'get her life back'.

What else could happen? Surely there wasn't anything that could eclipse the events of the previous seven weeks? Sadly there was.

On Monday, 1 June, the world awoke to the headline 'SuBo Taken to Priory'. Nothing more really needed to be said – although a lot more was going to be written – as that phrase said it all. 'The Hairy Angel,' 'Rambo', call her what you will, the woman who had enchanted the world and then caused it to examine its own motives for that fascination, was inside 'the clinic of the stars'.

The Priory group of hospitals was famous for its celebrity patients – Kate Moss, Ronnie Wood and Pete

Doherty had all been treated by them – and now Susan was joining the list. The final and the week leading up to it, let alone the worldwide spotlight she had been in since the start of April, all came together in one terrible, seemingly inevitable, collision.

The details of what happened to her don't make pleasant reading. And although she was to later explain them away by saying she was tired, they were still very worrying.

Show aides had contacted police to say she was acting strangely at her London hotel, the four-star Crowne Plaza in St James near Buckingham Palace, the Sunday after the contest. Paramedics arrived and helped the 'spaced out' star, who had been continually weeping that day, through the lobby and into an ambulance just after 6pm. At one stage she had apparently passed out in her room.

A Metropolitan Police Inspector and a police doctor were called to assist. The ambulance, tailed by a police car, then took her to the Priory in Southgate, north London.

A Scotland Yard spokeswoman said: 'Police were called at approximately 6pm to a central London hotel to doctors assessing a woman under the Mental Health Act. The woman was taken voluntarily by ambulance to a clinic. At the request of doctors, police accompanied the ambulance.'

Once she got there, reports said that she asked, 'Where's Pebbles?' and only calmed down when staff rang her home number so that she could leave a message for the cat. She was said to have been in a panic over her cat – which was being looked after by friends. One source said, 'Susan was distraught and convinced they'd taken her cat. She was crying she hadn't fed Pebbles and flapping her arms like a confused child. It was incredibly distressing. She was talking to herself then went quiet.'

The Priory clinic describes itself as 'a private hospital specialising in the treatment of mental health problems including addiction... For people suffering from mild to moderate mental health issues, such as stress and anxiety, the hospital provides a range of outpatient-based therapy services such as individual and group based Cognitive Behaviour Therapy. For those people requiring inpatient care for more severe psychiatric illness such as depression, psychotic illness or addiction, there are residential facilities for 52 patients. Priory has a highly experienced team of mental health professionals and support staff, which include consultant psychiatrists, psychologists, nurses and therapists.'

'She'd been at the hotel for a few days, but since Saturday's final had been acting strangely, causing a bit of a stir,' an insider at the Crowne Plaza said. 'The staff were concerned – something wasn't right. When the paramedics and police arrived she agreed to go voluntarily. She didn't make a fuss. The paramedics calmly took her out through the main lobby and into the waiting ambulance. It was all done very calmly. They didn't want to stress or upset her. She didn't look well – she looked lost, not all there.'

A spokesman for *Britain's Got Talent* said, 'Following Saturday's show, Susan is exhausted and emotionally drained.

'She has been seen by her private GP, who supports her decision to take a few days out for rest and recovery. We offer her our ongoing support and wish her a speedy recovery.

'It is a talent show at the end of the day and people are auditioning on their talent merits. There is no formal psychological testing at the beginning of the show. Compared with something like *Big Brother*, where you are looking at people going into a house for three months, the people on *Britain's Got Talent* have three or four performances maximum and spend only seven to 10 days in a hotel for the semi-finals and final. It is a very different scenario.

'But because of the level of media attention and the speed with which this has become a global phenomenon, we will be reviewing all of our policies in relation to psychological assessment.'

Details began to emerge of Susan's behaviour leading up to and after that final performance. A twisted section of the audience had booed her when Piers Morgan made her his tip to win and once she left the spotlight she had sunk into the arms of producers and buried her head in her hands before starting to cry. She had also allegedly uttered a four-letter outburst shortly before the show was due to start because her stage costume had not arrived.

In fairness to Susan, such a delay would have sent many a more experienced performer into a rage. She was ushered into a room by production staff, but insiders said she could still be heard 'swearing like a trooper'.

After returning to her dressing room once the verdict had been given and Diversity were pronounced the winner, she was widely reported to have shouted backstage: 'I hate this show. I hate it.'

She was also said to have burst out of her dressing room and run along a corridor with only her bra on her top half, yelling abuse at production staff before throwing a cup of water over a floor manager. And sources said that she had been introducing production staff to 'an invisible friend' and borrowing mobile phones to leave messages for Pebbles.

Irene Carter, the mother of one of the members of dance troupe Sugarfree from the contest, said, 'Susan was acting very strange all week. One time staff working on the show backstage asked if she was okay and she said she was talking to her friend.

'She then introduced everyone in the room to this "friend", who wasn't actually there. Another time she came up to my daughter Emma in the hotel and asked to borrow her mobile phone. She left this really bizarre message which went on for several minutes. When she got off the phone she said she had been talking to her cat back at home.

'Susan said she had to call Pebbles several times

throughout the day or she would miss her. I really think she was cracking up.'

Leaving messages for her cat was bizarre enough but talking to an imaginary friend? What was that all about? Psychologist Dr Lesley Perman-Kerr said, 'It seems that Susan Boyle was feeling very alone in a world she didn't really understand or connect with, and I think she must have been using this imaginary friend as a kind of escape. She may have been a little delusional as well.

'I think it's probably quite different to how children normally use imaginary friends because they are very imaginative and can dream up imaginary friends as play partners. Also they can use them to say things they want to say but want someone else to blame it on. Children can have imaginary friends if they are very stressed, but it's not anything similar to what she's doing. I suspect she's extremely stressed and simply unable to cope in the world she found herself in.'

Psychologist Linda Papadopoulos said, 'If Susan is feeling insecure, inventing an imaginary friend might be something she'd do.

'Lots of people talk to themselves to comfort themselves and lots of children do it at some point in their lives. I'm guessing that she feels a need for comfort when she's in a situation where she's feeling very anxious.

'When we're stressed out, we go to tried and tested techniques to cope.'

Professor Chris Thompson, director of healthcare

services at The Priory, said the intense public scrutiny she had faced in previous weeks could have triggered anxiety and depression which would need months of therapy.

'People are shocked to the core by the level of public scrutiny of them. Most of us go through life with very little feedback. When you start reading things about yourself you can start to think: "Is that who I really am?"' He also said that if an exhausted person continued without treatment they could develop anxiety or depression.

'It seems to me a bit like walking out on to a branch and then sawing it off behind you. The fact that Susan Boyle appears to have broken down in some way so close to the end of the series suggests there is a link. I would want to know that people being exposed to such pressures are given proper care.'

Professor Thompson went on to say, 'I cannot talk specifically about Susan Boyle, but any admission to a psychiatric hospital for a matter of days is, in my opinion, a failed admission, because either it was unnecessary in the first place or the job hasn't been done fully.'

He added, 'I would want to know that people being exposed to such pressures are actually looked after. I think I know what TV companies would say – they would say "these people are willing volunteers"... The fact that there is consent between the TV company and contestant does not prevent the TV company having a duty of care once that consent has been given.'

He stressed that the north London private clinic 'is not a rest home and it's not a spa. It is a psychiatric hospital.'

Susan's brother Gerry confirmed she was missing her home in West Lothian – and Pebbles. 'She is a bit tired and maybe even a wee bit homesick,' he revealed. 'When I spoke to her yesterday she was asking about her cat. It's going to take a wee while for her to get her head round all this because she just comes from a wee village in Blackburn.

'First and foremost we have to make sure she is happy, and she is – she wouldn't change all this for the world. It would be nice to get her back home for a couple of days. But she will bounce back – we know our Susan. She's at the Priory talking to people there about how she feels and where she goes from here. She sounded a bit happier, she sounded a bit more like herself, but certainly a bit more rested.

'She's been on a tremendous roller-coaster. There's been an enormous amount of media speculation and intense activity. She's not used to that. She's coming to terms with that now that she's no longer an anonymous face.

'I think what led up to it was the build-up to the show and just psyching herself up for that and then wondering after the show, "Where do I go now?"'

Mr Boyle added, 'This is the start of Susan's international career, now that the talent show is finished. She is not interested in money, she's not a material person, but what she is interested in is working with her idols and

I'm sure Mr Cowell will have a few people lined up. I was absolutely delighted with the result on Saturday. In my opinion, it's not about winning the competition, it's about where your career goes afterwards.'

The show's production company Talkback Thames said, 'We offer her our ongoing support and wish her a speedy recovery.'

So did one of Susan's compatriots. Fellow Scot, Prime Minister Gordon Brown, was being interviewed on television in the middle of the Priory drama, and he said, 'I hope Susan Boyle is OK because she is a really, really nice person. I spoke to Simon Cowell last night and Piers Morgan and wanted to be sure that she was OK.'

Piers Morgan, in fact, gave an insider's view of the torment that Susan was going through. In an article he wrote for the *Mail on Sunday* seven days after Susan was admitted to the Priory, he described the events leading up to that admission.

The day of the final he had asked her if she was okay on the telephone.

'"Not really," she said. "I've not had a good night's sleep all week, I haven't been eating much, and I'm really stressed out."

'"You've got your chance to show everyone what you can do tonight. This is it, Susan. This is your moment to have the last laugh."

'She laughed, "I don't feel much like laughing. There's so much pressure, I don't want to let anyone down."

'"You won't. You have inspired millions of people around the world with your singing, and you mustn't let a few silly headlines ruin it for you. You've enjoyed the show haven't you?"

'"Oh yes, of course. I've been living my dream." I believed her but was still worried for her.

'"You going to be OK tonight?" She didn't hesitate. "Yes."

'Later that night, Susan walked on to the stage and unleashed a magnificent new version of "I Dreamed A Dream". I was staggered by how confidently she sang. After the extraordinary rollercoaster she'd been through, I genuinely feared it might all end in tears at the final hurdle, that she might crack under the maelstrom of attention and expectation.

'But she didn't. She nailed it. To my shock and dismay, though, there were a few boos in the audience when I suggested in my critique that she should win the show.

'I realised then that she probably wouldn't win, that the bubble had indeed burst right at the last minute, that the British public – as Simon had feared – had grown a little bored and irritated by Boyle mania...'

Morgan continued: 'And Susan was fantastically generous and modest in defeat, while reserving the right to do one last wiggle on stage.

'The next day, I was asked to call Susan because she was "exhausted and upset". We spoke for half an hour, and she admitted, "I'm so tired, I need to get away from all this for a while."

'"You were brilliant last night," I said. "I didn't win, though. Will I still be able to have a career as a singer?"

'"Of course you will," I replied, truthfully. "And remember that your dream was never to win this show, it was to sing professionally."

'"That's true, it is. It's all I have ever wanted to do."

'She was undeniably jittery and erratic in that conversation. There was laughter and tears, excitement and sadness. She had been through an unprecedented two months.

'"Are you glad you came on the show?" I asked.

'"I am," she said. "Even the way I feel now, I am."'

Morgan was to add elsewhere, 'It is probably a good thing all round that Susan didn't win and can be under the radar for a bit. It is not a very serious matter, she is just exhausted and needs some rest.'

That view was echoed by Amanda Holden, who said in a television interview, 'I understand that we've spoken to her doctors and they really have reassured us that there are no underlying mental issues and it is purely just that she's knackered, for want of a better word.

'And I think as we all keep saying, to have been thrust into such a media circus for seven weeks – it's hard enough for me, Piers and Simon to deal with, let alone somebody that's had absolutely no experience.'

She defended the way contestants for the show were

assessed and said more psychological screenings of contestants would be impractical. 'You can't kind of give every single person who's just an auditioner that kind of long-winded attention,' she told *GMTV*.

'But I think that what was done for Susan was the right thing to have done. I know that they've kind of checked her out and they've spoken to people in her village and there was no reason that we needed to check her for anything else, and I still agree with that.

'All these shows take great care, and there are rules and standards that we all have to stick by. And I know that we care very much about Susan and so the right people are looking after her now.'

And she was to add, 'It's taken its toll on her. She's gone from a woman who nobody knew to worldwide fame. For anybody in the business to handle that kind of stress is an enormous pressure and she probably has just crumbled under it. She will just need some time to recuperate, to rest. Actually, it's probably a blessing that she didn't win because the spotlight's not so heavily on her.'

Scotland's First Minister Alex Salmond, who had been sending messages of good luck to Susan during the past weeks, was also concerned, saying *BGT* should 'probably' take better care of its contestants.

He told BBC Radio Scotland's 'Morning Extra' that Boyle's performance in Saturday's final, after weeks of intense media scrutiny, was a 'triumph'.

'I'm just wondering, could anybody really stand up to

that sort of pressure, particularly when you're not used to it, and not have a few difficulties with it?' he said. 'Does that mean we shouldn't have shows like that? No, I think that show, *Britain's Got Talent*, gives people an opportunity and a chance and I doubt you would find a contestant who said, "No, I didn't want to have a go and take my chance." Should they take care of their contestants a bit better? Yes, they probably should.'

Susan's brother Gerry's views that weekend were different. 'They just left her on her own. She has got a short fuse and she just blew. Who wouldn't under that pressure? She's told me, "I feel tired and stressed," and that's understandable. The people at *Britain's Got Talent* have been guilty of not dealing properly with a situation that's quite unique. You have to remember she's had to deal with television and the press, which she's never done before, on her own. They should have done a better job. They sent her into the lions' den totally unprepared. They shoved her out there and made her accessible and then sat back and watched while they got free publicity.'

He added, after she was taken to The Priory, 'She started feeling extremely anxious on Sunday afternoon. Later that day she had what you and I would call a panic attack. She has been away from home all week and was very lonely and in all honesty very homesick. Susan panicked because the show had come to an end and she did not know what the future held for her. There are no contracts on the table and she hadn't spoken to Cowell properly.'

Gerry did subsequently remark, after Susan had time to settle in at The Priory, 'She sounded a bit happier, she sounded a bit more like herself, but certainly a bit more rested and she seems to be coming home.

'I think her friends in America would call this an anxiety attack. She's been on a tremendous rollercoaster. There's been an enormous amount of media speculation and intense activity.

'She's not used to that. She's coming to terms with that now that she's no longer an anonymous face. I think what led up to it was the build-up to the show and just psyching herself up for that and then wondering after the show "where do I go now?".'

Brother John commented, 'The past six weeks have been a dream for her but also very tiring. I fully expect her to be back home in a couple of days and playing with her cat.

'She is a very highly strung lady and she feels like she's let people down. But it is a nonsense. She needs a good rest and reassurance that her future is guaranteed. Six weeks ago it was a dream and it still is a dream and it's come true.

'She feels like she has let Blackburn down. She definitely hasn't, but that is obviously what she thinks. She is worried about how people will feel about her. She doesn't realise how much people love her.

'This is the best place for her. She is exhausted, but she is doing fine and needs her family and friends around her.'

But it wasn't just those who were close to *BGT* or Susan who had views on her condition and the effect her fame had had on her.

Messages of support flooded in from 'ordinary' people around the world, worried about her health and her state of mind, as well as from those in the public eye. In addition, there were many better-informed on the pressures she had been under, who too were concerned.

Mark Borkowski, the publicist and author of *The Fame Formula: How Hollywood's Fixers, Fakers and Star Makers Created the Celebrity Industry*, said, 'This is the modern equivalent of a freak show. I'm one of the few people who didn't feel that she had much of a future. You can't pluck somebody with those issues and fix them overnight... We are beginning to see more and more people who are casualties of the process.'

He added, 'When you need to buy time, you shove someone in The Priory. They want this woman to be fit and are hoping she will come through the other side. If they get this right, she could make millions. But at what personal cost?'

Amy Clarke of Mencap – the highly-respected charity for those with learning difficulties and their families – said, 'Sometimes people with a learning disability, like me, find it harder to communicate and get used to new things. Susan Boyle's life has changed overnight and she, like anyone else, should have the right support to deal with this kind of pressure. Someone with a learning disability might need support dealing with new situations and communicating their feelings in an appropriate way.'

But she also said, 'I like the fact that someone with a learning disability has done well on a talent show. Susan Boyle is an inspiration to me because you rarely see people with a learning disability on television and making a success in showbiz.'

Andrew McCulloch, chief executive of the Mental Health Foundation, said, 'As a result of taking part in *Britain's Got Talent*, Susan Boyle has received an unprecedented amount of attention. Considering that she has also had to cope with the pressure of taking part in a national television competition it is understandable that Susan is feeling exhausted. The experience can be overwhelming, especially for somebody who is not used to living in the spotlight. Reality television programmes and the media can very quickly propel people who lead very ordinary lives into a world that is unfamiliar and fast-paced. It is only right that Susan is being supported at this time and is getting the care she needs.'

The debate came as a survey of more than 3,000 Britons found that seven out of ten people believed Susan should not have been allowed to perform, while six out of ten said ITV exploited her to bolster viewing numbers.

Media regulator Ofcom received a 'large number of

complaints' about the situation. Section eight of the broadcasting code states: 'People in a state of distress should not be put under pressure to take part in a programme or provide interviews, unless it is warranted.' But the *Britain's Got Talent* production company said no pressure had been put on Susan to perform in the final; it had been entirely her decision.

The row continued and Culture Secretary Andy Burnham questioned whether TalkbackThames and ITV had exercised their 'duty of care' towards Susan. Mr Burnham said there should be a 'process of discussion' with ITV in order to establish what happened but emphasised broadcasters must take care of people such as Susan. 'We are living in a world where it is not just about what happens on telly on a Saturday night. There is 360-degree scrutiny, 365 days a year. We need to look after people, not just around the camera. Broadcasters should always put people's welfare first.'

Three days after being taken to The Priory, brother Gerry was able to announce that Susan was 'coming back to her old ways', although she was still said to be worried that her career might be over before it had started. 'Where does her career go from here? Will she be still accepted? She didn't win the competition. Will people still want to hear her sing? And will there be a career for her as we stand here today? What Susan needs most now is to return from London to Edinburgh, to come home to Blackburn, be at home for a couple of days.'

After five days at The Priory, five days in which the world in general, and Britain and America in particular, waited with baited breath for news of her welfare, it was revealed that Susan had at last left the hospital although not even her family seemed to know exactly where she'd gone.

'I think things are becoming clearer now and she's much more content. I believe she's in the middle of London, in a flat in London,' Gerry told *GMTV*.

'The way forward now is to talk about where her career goes from here. She's absorbing the fact that America has a huge appetite for her and she's now beginning to believe that yes, indeed, I will be a singer and there will be a recording career beyond it. It's all she ever wanted to do.

'Simon Cowell – he's been around the dance floor a few times hasn't he? I'm sure he knows that he's got someone who has broken down the barriers in America before she even gets there and I'm sure Simon will do a good job for her.'

Whatever kind of treatment it was deemed Susan needed, one of the first sightings of her came when she indulged in some good old-fashioned retail therapy. It wasn't in the boutiques of South Molton Street, W1, or the department stores of Knightsbridge, however, that she decided to splash out. Rather it was in the quiet, suburban town of Radlett in Hertfordshire, an affluent area popular for its mix of countryside and ease of access to London.

Susan was joined on her shopping trip by Dr Sarah Lotzof, a private doctor with an interest in psychiatry. When asked how she was feeling, Susan replied, 'Oh fine, thanks.' And when complimented on her appearance, she just smiled coyly and thanked well-wishers. The pair went to the Lulu & Fred clothes store in Radlett. Staff closed the shop so Susan could browse in privacy, and she bought a range of expensive clothes from designers such as Handwritten, Elie Tahari and Twin-Set. Her spree included stocking up on casual wear, smart trousers, matching tops, cardigans, shoes and a dress. Frederic Benisty, co-owner of the shop, said, 'She was here having a good time. She came out with her doctor and you can imagine that when someone like that goes out they are going to be a little bit anxious. But halfway through she was absolutely thrilled and happy. She was absolutely fine. She was joking around and having a laugh.'

By the Saturday, seven days after the exhausting final, Susan was looking happy and healthy when she flew into Edinburgh Airport from London. She smiled and posed before a 'welcome home' sign before being whisked off for a planned family reunion at a secret location.

Brother John said, 'I have spoken to Susan and she is very excited and positive about the future. She told me, "Don't worry. I'm having the time of my life." She said she felt fantastic and couldn't wait to come back home this weekend. She was giggling away and sounded more relaxed than she has in ages.

'That's the thing with Susan. She suffers from these mood swings, so I hope that now she's out of the clinic she's OK.

'I also hope she's been reassured by Simon Cowell's people that everything's on track with her career and that she can now start looking forward.'

He said his sister had been pleased when Cowell rang her at The Priory to reassure her that her career was on track. 'By all accounts it gave her a real boost and I hope that I can thank him soon for all the help he's given her,' he said. But he added, 'She was put under extreme pressure and I don't think they handled the situation well. These were exceptional circumstances and they had a duty of care towards her.

'I'm very angry about it. They could have done more to help Susan. She can be very influenced by other people. She never listens to her family. It's part of her slight disability. She's very naive,' he said.

Brother Gerry also highlighted some of her difficulties. 'She thinks the best of everyone – that's her upbringing, she takes everyone at face value. A part of her thinks she can walk down the street and nothing is different to before. But it's not like that any more – she's a worldwide phenomenon. We just hope she doesn't get taken for a ride by unscrupulous people.'

Gerry said first thing she planned do with her earnings was to buy her £80,000 four-bedroom council home in Blackburn. It had been rented by her family for 50 years and SuBo still slept in the same room she had as a child. 'She will keep the house as part of the family and if she can afford a bigger house she will buy that too. She's certainly not going to buy a Jaguar or do this and that and fritter the money away – she can't even drive! That's her all over – she's so generous. Money is not really important to her. What she wants is a successful singing career and to be respected.'

If one aspect of the torment she had been through was her separation from Pebbles that at least was to end. The much-loved pet was shielded from photographers – one newspaper decided 'Pebbles Has a Minder' – while being carried from Susan's home to be reunited with her at a secret address.

By the middle of the week, ten days after the collapse at the hotel, Susan was winging her way back down to London for rehearsals for the *Britain's Got Talent* tour. The question was, would she be fit enough to appear?

One insider said, 'Everything depends on Susan and how she feels. We have made it clear that we are in her hands and we just want to make sure that she is fit and well.

'At the moment it looks like Susan will join the rest of the *BGT* finalists on stage on some of the dates, but she won't do the entire tour. The details are still being worked out. Susan is most excited about starting work on her album and we have a responsibility to make sure she is cared for and is happy and well.'

Susan was in good spirits after she jetted into London, waving and dancing for photographers. She wore the same cardigan, trousers and necklace that she had worn while shopping in Radlett the previous Friday and to travel home to Scotland the next day. Despite buying those new clothes, this made it three appearances in the same combination in less than a week. Perhaps the fact that Pebbles had also been brought to London to accompany played a part in her apparent good humour. She also knew that she could contact Dr Lotzof any time if a problem developed.

Simon Cowell reportedly paid for her accommodation on her return – a luxury flat valued at £2 million in a converted convent in North London, which also had the essential requirement that the letting agents would allow a cat to be kept there.

It was also widely reported that U2's financial wizard Ossie Kilkenny, 62, had agreed to mastermind Susan's career.

The other acts would be staying in hotels, but the plan was that Susan would be returned to her new home whenever possible. No less than four limos were to be used to fool photographers so that her comings and goings could be kept as secret as possible.

Susan was due to rehearse on the Tuesday for the opening night of the month-long 26-show tour in Birmingham that Friday, but she cancelled, causing many to wonder whether she would make it. But make it she did, and in style.

The *Daily Express* announced:

'Susan Boyle made a sensational return to the stage last night – winning a standing ovation from thousands of fans. She looked relaxed and happy on the opening night of the *Britain's Got Talent* tour in Birmingham. Wearing the same silver gown she wore in the controversial final, she sang a stunning rendition of "I Dreamed A Dream".

'Her assured performance and good spirits allayed fears about her just a week after she checked out of a London clinic... Last night, as the 5,000-strong crowd called out for more, she blew them a kiss.

'Host Stephen Mulhern joked that her cat Pebbles – nearly as famous as the Scottish spinster herself – couldn't make the show because he was in Las Vegas.'

The Times reported:

'Susan Boyle returned to the stage last night after keeping her fans waiting over whether she would perform on the opening night of the *Britain's Got Talent* live tour. The Scottish singer performed at the National Indoor Arena in Birmingham less than two weeks after she was admitted to the Priory clinic. She had lost to the dance group Diversity in the final of the ITV show.

'Tour organisers are determined not to put any pressure on Boyle to perform in case she suffers a repeat of the emotional breakdown that led to her admission to the north London hospital. As the singer arrived in Birmingham she told well-wishers: "I'm feeling much

SUSAN BOYLE – LIVING THE DREAM

better now, thank you, and I'm really looking forward to performing." But organisers said that she was leaving the decision until the last minute.

'In the event, she took to the stage, belting out the hits "I Dreamed A Dream" and "Memory" from the musicals *Les Misérables* and *Cats*. During the performance she blew a kiss to her fans as they screamed and whistled.

'The fans who queued outside the 13,000-capacity venue had been left with no information as to whether the woman most of them had come to see would take the stage.'

Critic Kevin O'Sullivan of the *Sunday Mirror* wrote: 'No word of a lie… the first night of the *Britain's Got Talent* live tour was one of the most exhilarating experiences of my life. Amazing!

'Whisper it quietly – but it was even more fun than the sensational TV show. No boring judges to listen to. The winners Diversity were astonishing. These guys can dance like nobody else.

'But let's cut to the chase. The 5,000 ecstatic fans who turned Birmingham's NIA stadium into a seething cauldron of excitement couldn't wait for a certain Susan Boyle. And, after a week of "Would she or wouldn't she turn up", she did. Better still, she didn't disappoint. It's ridiculous pretending that the spinster from Blackburn, West Lothian is the greatest singer in the world. But, now that she's the most hit-upon YouTube phenomenon of all time, she has an aura about her.

'SuBo's got charisma. And she knows how to use it. Did she nail all the notes? No. Did she know how to bring the house down? Oh yes!

'She didn't get a standing ovation ... she got a jump up and down, hold your hands in the air, raise the roof roar of approval.'

The *BGT* tour host, Stephen Mulhern, had to admit, 'She did great – an amazing comeback and the audience loved it. But I honestly didn't know if she was going to go on stage, right until the last minute. I was worried I would say her name, turn around and not see her there. I had some ad-libs ready.

'I was told 20 minutes before she performed that she was coming on. But when I went on stage to introduce her I was still unsure. I was worried I might say her name and she wouldn't be there. I think that's the way it's going to be for the rest of the tour.' Stephen said he had 'absolutely no idea' whether she would be able to complete the tour or keep up her dazzling performances.

'Susan was scared backstage,' he said. 'She was nervous. But when she did get on to stage she did brilliantly.'

So the 'comeback' had been a triumph. There were reviews so filled with superlatives that many artists would spend a lifetime performing and never come near such praise.

Yet, as with so many aspects of Susan's life, there were many more twists to come.

CHAPTER ELEVEN
ON THE ROAD

Birmingham had been a triumph but the second date of the tour, at Sheffield, never quite reached the same level of excellence or praise.

True, Susan received a standing ovation, but she also appeared to stumble over the words of, of all songs, 'Memory'.

Susan, who had taken to wearing her late mother Bridget's wedding ring around her neck as a memento to give her strength, seemed to lose her way briefly as she sang the *Cats* showstopper but was cheered on by the crowd at the Sheffield Arena. Earlier in the show, however, she received a mixed reaction from the audience, with several people booing when her name was announced.

Wearing a long sequined silver dress, she appeared in the second half of the show and began her performance with 'Memory', before launching into 'I Dreamed A

Dream'. She thanked the audience as they stood and cheered in support as she stumbled over the words to 'Memory'; both songs received a standing ovation and she blew a kiss and waved at her fans.

The third city on the tour was Manchester and Susan pulled out of her two scheduled performances. A tour insider said, 'There is nothing sinister going on. It's been very much one step at a time.' And a spokesman said, 'She sends her sincere apologies to her fans for not appearing.'

That left a big question mark over whether or not she would make it for the next scheduled stop on the tour. And that, of all places, happened to be Glasgow. Such was the world's interest in Susan that her appearances or non-appearances were big news all around the world. From Australia to America, the Far East to the Frozen North, the public were being informed of which shows she made, and what the performance was like, and which ones she didn't, and why.

Piers Morgan explained, 'Susan is fine – she just did three shows then felt too tired. She has doctors with her all the time. I know she really wants to sing in Scotland. I think that's one of the reasons she took a rest, but they will take a decision each day about whether she will perform. As far as I'm aware she is absolutely fine, just a bit tired.'

Perhaps it's worth noting the brief list of 'current people news briefs' that Reuters News Agency circulated on 16 June. There was a story about vegetarian Paul

McCartney launching a 'meat free Monday', American talk-show host David Letterman apologising for a sexually charged joke he had made about a woman politician, a member of Aerosmith rejoining the band after injuring his head climbing out of his Ferrari, and the latest in the row over Madonna's adoption of an African child.

Four big names: an ex-Beatle, a gigantic rock band, the most famous chat show host in the States and the most commercially successful woman singer of all time. All of them were mentioned in the stories that circulated around the globe. But the lead story? Yes, it was Susan.

Back where it all began, Glasgow's SECC, she entered to thunderous cheers and chants of 'Susan! Susan!' Her hair, now darker than it had originally been, was immaculate and she wore a shimmering grey dress.

Stephen Mulhern introduced her by saying, 'Now it's time to welcome the most Googled lady on earth. The world's talking about one lady. This lady.'

The 9000-strong crowd at the SECC were on their feet as Susan walked on stage.

Although her semi-final performance of 'Memory' and her rendition of the same song at Sheffield both had their faults, this time she was perfect. As she finished there was a roar from the crowd, which continued as she moved into 'I Dreamed A Dream', and with another ovation her confidence showed and she waved to the crowd.

Mulhern said, 'You are definitely the best audience we've had.'

One report of the show said: 'Show-stopper Susan Boyle was met with rapturous applause as she took to the stage in front of a home crowd.

'There had been doubts as to whether the now world-famous singer from West Lothian would perform in the *Britain's Got Talent* live show in Glasgow last night after pulling out of the event in Manchester. But the plucky church worker wowed the crowds as she belted out "I Dreamed a Dream", the song which made her a global superstar.

'Scots' fans will be hoping Boyle can repeat her dazzling performance when the show reaches the Edinburgh Playhouse tonight.

'Not only did she receive a standing ovation at the end of the Glasgow gig, the packed hall took to their feet as she walked on to the stage in a floor-length sparkling dress and twice during her performance.

'Many fans were waving homemade banners; some said, "We love you Susan" and "Susan is the best".

'One fan, Bryan Felvus, 23, from Motherwell in Lanarkshire, said, "She was brilliant. She had to be here tonight. She was great and deserved every bit of support she got and she got the loudest cheer of the evening."

'Another, Audrey Hinde, 39, from Ayrshire said, "I thought she was fantastic. She brought tears to my eyes. She didn't seem under pressure at all." Last night Boyle, from the village of Blackburn, rose to the occasion and once again wowed the crowds.'

But the controversy over whether Susan should be experiencing this strain, whether she should have been put through the ordeal of competing in the final in the first place, would not go away. It was a source of fierce debate, so much so that Simon Cowell felt he had to explain the background to it.

'I sat down with her and said, "Look, if this is getting too much for you, you don't have to go into the final, no one's going to force you."

'I told her family, "I'll rip the contract up, you can have it back. I'll do whatever Susan wants." She looked me in the eye and said, "No, I want to win this competition. I want to give it a go." It was only at the moment she lost when it hits you and you go, "How are you going to cope with this?" She found it very, very difficult.

'No one put a gun to her head and said you've got to enter this show. She got in a fragile state because she couldn't cope with all the attention. That's what you can't predict.

'But for me to have said on that first day, "Susan, I'm going to make a decision about you and say you can't cope with this, so you can't live your dream" – I've got no right to say that.'

Next stop was Edinburgh and brother Gerry said, 'She has been ringing around family members to ensure they are in the audience tonight. She sounds fine and happy. She's like a kid in a sweetie shop. She's really looking forward to singing in her home territory. She was very keen to get back to performing. It's just about pacing it and giving her a rest when she needs it.

'This is what she always wanted to do. She loves entertaining the public. She is very keen to get on with her recording career afterwards. She'll be ringing round the family, seeing who can make it tonight. I'm sure there'll be quite a few there.'

The show at the Edinburgh Playhouse was sold out and many of Susan's friends and neighbours in Blackburn missed out on tickets.

Jackie Russell, from Happy Valley Hotel in Blackburn, said, 'I think a lot of people were disappointed. Everybody wanted to go and see her, but I think it's fully booked now. It was very hard to get tickets.

'I'm worried it's all getting a little too much for Susan. People don't realise she's just a local girl from an ex-mining village, who's been thrust into the limelight. I'm not surprised she's exhausted – it's been exhausting for us with all the attention we've had.

'I'm sure Susan will be back in to sing here, but it could be a long time. I've got about 500 cards and letters to give her – everyone has been giving them to me.'

The Boyles and their friends weren't the only ones eager to see Susan. Lisa Carpinello, 49, and her daughter Courtney, 12, travelled from Philadelphia, America, to see Susan in action. 'My husband has had to listen to "I Dreamed a Dream" for a month solid and he insisted I come over,' Lisa said. 'We stayed in Blackburn so we could go to the Happy Valley bar where she used to sing.'

Susan's appearance in Edinburgh, too, was a triumph. One review said:

'Sparkling in the simple silver dress that took her to second place in the *Britain's Got Talent* final just three weeks ago, Susan Boyle clocked up three standing ovations for a rapturous nine-minute homecoming performance at the Edinburgh Playhouse last night.

'In her first local appearance since leaving West Lothian for stardom in London, the 48-year-old singer perfectly performed two of the stage tunes that helped to make her the biggest internet phenomenon on the planet.

'While she was on stage only long enough to perform her songs and take a bow, her stunning vocal talent more than made up for her low-key appearance.'

Afterwards, her spokeswoman declared the performance had been a resounding return to form, but warned Boyle's fans that she would need rest days in order to cope with the demands of touring. 'We've not toured with her before so don't know how many performances she can cope with. We are waiting for her to tell us when she needs a rest.'

A report also said: 'Boyle was last night at number three on the Playhouse's post-interval bill, just after a performance by last year's winner George Sampson, and her arrival on stage took the excited audience by surprise.

'Surrounded on all sides by the deafening roar of screams and applause from the crowd, an apprehensive Boyle walked out to meet the microphone in the centre of the stage as the giant screen behind her projected highlights of her time on the ITV show that made her a household name.'

Singing with warmth and clarity, any doubts about Boyle's health and ability to perform after her recent spell in the Priory were quickly overcome as she easily drowned out the calls of the enthusiastic crowd with pitch perfect high notes in an almost flawless vocal performance. Offering the audience a hint of the cheeky smile that had captured the world she began to visibly relax on stage. Stepping back to the microphone she then delivered her most confident performance of the night.

Singing the *Les Misérables hit*, 'I Dreamed A Dream', made famous on You Tube after her first audition in Glasgow, Boyle gave a rendition so moving it that some said it 'would put idol Elaine Paige to shame.'

But if Edinburgh was a triumph, the show at Liverpool on 18 June wasn't. Susan didn't make the show after reportedly being found clinging to a hotel balcony screaming, 'Where's my cat?'

She was spotted in a distressed state on the interior balcony outside her room in Liverpool's four-star Radisson Blu Hotel, shouting down at the reception area, looking for her beloved cat Pebbles.

An eyewitness said, 'She was not in a good shape. All she kept shouting was, "I want my cat... I NEED my cat!" It was very surreal. I think people just felt sorry for her because she was clearly unhappy.'

About half an hour later, minders ushered her down the hotel's fire escape to a loading area at the back to avoid waiting press and fans. Shortly after she was driven away, organisers announced she would yet again miss one of the *BGT* tour shows.

She should have been one of the stars at Liverpool's 11,000-seater Echo Arena but many thought she had not looked well when she arrived in the city around 2pm.

An onlooker said, 'She just did not look right. She arrived in a Mercedes but as soon as she got out she ran away from the fans and the photographers. She just seemed to bolt but then she got stuck in the hotel's revolving doors which looked ridiculous. She was acting really weird. When she was at reception waiting to be booked in, she just stood there scratching her belly with her top pulled up. She was out of it.'

A spokeswoman for Susan said that she was unaware of the incident on the balcony but said there were no plans for a return to the Priory. 'Susan is not ill and I am not aware of any problems. She is just tired at the moment. She is going back down to London to have a sleep and a bit of a rest,' she added.

Susan pulled out of the next concert at the Cardiff Arena and a spokesman passed on a message – 'Sorry, to all her fans', adding, 'She would love to be able to perform every single evening but she is aware of what she can and can't do. I feel sorry for her because she doesn't want to let people down but also she needs to have a rest.'

Susan then missed two performances in Nottingham before returning to the stage for two dates at London's Wembley Arena, where she sang her customary two songs and received a standing ovation. She pledged not to miss the next gig, in Aberdeen, and flew up to wow the crowd.

Given her 'no-shows' so far on the tour, it was no surprise that there were doubts within the local community as to whether she would appear. But appear she did, arriving in a silver Mercedes at 6pm.

A review of her performance noted: 'In a glittering grey dress, perfectly made-up face and sleek hairstyle, the woman who might be on the brink of making a fortune looked a million dollars.

'Screaming fans jumped to their feet in a standing ovation as she belted out the song that first rocketed her into the headlines – "I Dreamed a Dream" and then the haunting "Memory".

'In spite of reports she was still behaving erratically, she looked calm and seemed to enjoy every second of her performance.'

The roadshow eventually hit Dublin and then Belfast. Susan dedicated her performance at Dublin's O2 Arena to her mother Bridget, both her parents having come from Keadue in Co. Donegal. No doubt it was an emotional return to Ireland for Susan, who had often travelled to Knock, where she first performed on Irish soil as part of a parish pilgrimage to a shrine to the Virgin Mary. 'I knew it was something I had to do. I had to get on with it. That's where the courage came from, my mother,' she said.

There were 20 dates on the tour, several of which had matinee performances too, and it took the *BGT* cast the length and breadth of England, Scotland, Ireland and Wales. Despite what people were hearing, the surprising aspect was that, in spite of the tentative start, Susan managed to make an appearance – normally to a tumultuous reception – on most of those dates, a remarkable achievement given her fragile state of mind just days prior to the tour beginning. It was an achievement in itself.

CHAPTER TWELVE
LIVING THE DREAM

One day in June, just before the *Britain's Got Talent* tour was about to start, Susan was sitting in Simon Cowell's office. 'He asked me how I was doing and I said my dream was to record an album,' she revealed. 'He said, "If that's still what you want to do I will help you – but only if you promise to take it slowly." We did a try-out in the studio – I finally felt happy there. Everything I'd ever dreamed of was happening.'

By the first week in July, as the much-published tour, with its dramas and uncertainties, neared its end, Cowell was in a position to announce: 'I've cut one track with her and she sounds fantastic on record – she's so good, the album is not just going to be show tunes, we're going to take our time with this.'

Susan was happy and enjoying being in the studio, he said. Although he refused to say what the track they'd recorded was, Cowell added, 'It's not an obvious record but so far, it's good. She's got a really good recording voice.'

The song was actually 'Cry Me a River', the 1953 ballad that had been sung by Ella Fitzgerald, Joe Cocker and Michael Bublé but which had been made famous by Julie London. It also happened to be the song that Susan had recorded for charity back in 1999.

'She's happy and I think she's enjoying the process. Luckily, things have quietened down a bit,' Cowell said.

They may have 'quietened down' to some extent, but it was hard to notice from the outside. Susan was making her prime time debut in America – the key evening hours when viewing is at its peak – on NBC at the end of July. It was considered so important that President Obama's planned live press conference on his plans for health care had to be re-arranged so as not to interfere with it. The conference was moved forward an hour so that the 9pm slot was available for Susan.

The interview, conducted via a video link to Susan's London residence, was with Meredith Vieira, one of the leading personalities in American television. In common with many Americans, Vieira seemed to have an almost reverential feeling towards Susan.

'I'm one of those millions of people that fell in love with you in mid-April... You look gorgeous,' she gushed. 'I'm loving the hair... it's a little bit different, right, you got a slight little makeover?'

Susan's hair had been slightly cut and coloured, her eyebrows were trimmed and she was wearing a flattering purple knee-length dress. 'Just a slight one. I brush up quite well,' Susan replied.

'You do brush up very, very well. The journey you have been on. Everybody around the world suddenly saying, "Who is this Susan Boyle?" Are you having a good time?'

'It's just been unbelievable,' Susan replied. 'It's indescribable. It's a bit like being plucked from obscurity.'

'If she were here now, what do you think she would say to you?' Vieira asked Boyle, in a reference to Susan's mother. 'Susan, keep going,' Susan replied. And when Vieira said, 'Keep going?' Susan elaborated with '"Keep going – you're doing really well." That's what she'd say.'

Talking of her motivation, Susan added, 'I was a little girl. I had to get up there and prove to everybody that I could do it. So I applied for *Britain's Got Talent* and the rest you know.'

'Yeah, the rest of the world knows, actually,' Vieira smiled.

Vieira wanted Susan to describe 'just how overwhelming' it had all been and Susan told her, 'It felt like a giant demolition ball.' 'It felt like a demolition ball?' the interviewer asked. 'The impact. It was like a demolition ball,' Susan replied. 'It's been a rollercoaster.'

NBC had even arranged for Donny Osmond to make an appearance with a video message for Susan, and she then spoke live on air to her idol, Elaine Paige. 'I'm absolutely gobsmacked,' quipped Susan.

She had come across well, especially given the obvious clash of cultures: the ultra-smooth machine that is American entertainment television and the newcomer to this different, alien world. It was also the first time she had been interviewed since she had been admitted to the Priory, so her replies and attitude were even more commendable bearing that fact in mind.

Although Susan's appearance had changed considerably since that January audition, her assessment of it – that she 'brushed up well' – was pretty near the mark. But she was to step up a league with her next move.

Harpers Bazaar is one of the most famous magazines in the world. Its name is synonymous with elegant, attractive women in sophisticated surroundings. The list of supermodels and film stars who have graced its pages over the years is endless. So no wonder it made news when it was announced that Susan was to appear in the September issue.

The photoshoot took place at Cliveden, the Italianate stately-home in Buckinghamshire, which was now a five-star hotel. Home to the high-rollers of the so-called 'Cliveden Set' in the 1920s and 30s, it also featured in the 1960s Profumo scandal that involved politicians and call-girls.

'The idea behind the shoot was a very, very simple one,' Laura Brown, *Harpers*' special projects editor, said. 'It was to take gorgeous, glamorous and sensitive portraits of her. This was her first magazine photo shoot, so you can't do too much too soon.'

A made-over Susan was to be featured in various designer outfits in a spread called *Susan Boyle: Unsung Hero*.

'She came onto the stage and just transfixed us all. She's become a hero to a lot of people with dreams of stardom, or who maybe have a talent but have been too scared to express it.' Brown said Susan was 'comfortable and confident' during the shoot. 'I think Susan is getting more and more used to being in the spotlight and being on television and being photographed. Since April, you've seen her look day to day become more polished and refined. And she's growing in her confidence with what she'll wear and how she'll be perceived.'

The editor said that Susan said didn't undergo any radical makeover for the *Harpers* photo shoot. 'What we did on our shoot was give her a little bit of a haircut, and that was it, and a little bit of a curl. And actually the shape of her hair is great. She's got a really lovely curl to it. So we just tidied it up a little bit and paired it with some natural makeup, and she looked great.'

Susan was dressed in a 'mixture of designer and sort of high-street clothing' to reflect her style and personality. 'You don't want to put her into a crazy couture dress. I think she would feel very uncomfortable and it would look fraudulent,' Brown revealed.

In the most glamorous shot, Susan was pictured at a piano wearing a full-length black Tadashi Shoji gown. 'Another one of my favourite pictures has her in a really classic, beautiful purple Michael Kors long-sleeved dress with a really groovy, fun J.Crew necklace,' Brown said. 'And you can tell from the photograph that she looks really confident and she feels really great.'

Susan was also photographed in a bright blue classic trench coat over a silky green top and black skirt, and a long-sleeved, black sequined Donna Karan sweater. Susan joked on the photo set, 'It really made me feel like a Hollywood actress. Had my hair done up.'

Brown said Susan was always the first to crack a joke. 'Her laugh is quite genius, actually; it's got a real robust Scottish cackle to it. When you hear that laugh, I think everybody just lights up.'

Susan told the magazine, 'It does feels unreal. It will take a bit of adjusting to as I've led a sheltered life. Mentally I have to adjust. But it's all good. It was good, but overwhelming. It was too big for anyone to handle.'

Asked if she was glad she had auditioned, she grinned and said, 'It goes without saying. Come on, now!'

It wasn't all photo-shoots at stately homes, though. As that and the recording continued there were reports that Susan was planning to buy her Blackburn home which, with a discount because she had lived there for so long, would mean the asking price would be around £30,000. By this time Susan was living in a cream-painted

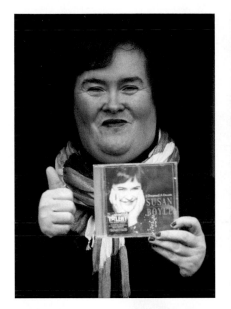

Above left and right: Susan's first album, *I Dreamed A Dream*, stormed the charts and went straight to number 1. © *PA Photos*

Below: Susan performs to fans in New York after securing worldwide success. © *NBCUPHOTOBANK/Rex Features*

Susan's fame grows as she appears in Paris in December 2009.

The epitome of the American Dream – SuBo arriving in Los Angeles to perform on the final of *America's Got Talent*.

The global hype around Susan Boyle continues to grow as swarms of paparazzi and fans wait to greet her wherever she goes.   © *Rex Features*

The pressure of fame became too much for Susan after her meteoric
rise to stardom, and she was treated in The Priory clinic in the summer
of 2009. © *PA Photos*

A simpler time for Susan, just as she was on the cusp of becoming a global superstar.

© *Tina Norris/Rex Features*

Above left and right: Her name in lights – Susan appears on US channel NBC's 'People of the Year' show.   © *NBCUPHOTOBANK/Rex Features*

Below: Susan performs to thousands of American fans in New York.

© *PA Photos*

The Susan Boyle fans
worldwide know and love.
© Erik Pendzich/Rex Features

apartment in Kensington, with Pebbles of course, with minimal, expensive furniture. She enjoyed living in what she referred to as her 'posh' pad and would make light-hearted references to her stardom.

She also had a PA to manage her diary and keep her company and a housekeeper to stock up on food and drink and keep Pebbles company when Susan was away.

Although she was spending more time in London, she was spotted going into the Royal Bank of Scotland's branch in Bathgate with a smile on her face (there had been reports that the album might earn her £5 million) and she chatted and waved to fans outside the branch.

One onlooker said, 'Susan looked on top of the world. She was waving and smiling at fans and looked fit and relaxed. She didn't appear to have a care in the world. It was really good to see her looking so well. Maybe she had just checked her bank statement!'

There were also plans being discussed by the local council to erect a life-size statue to her at a cost of £30,000 – the same price as her house – in Blackburn, and possibly even have a 'heritage trail' of some sort. If it ever came to fruition it would consist of her home, the nearby chip shop, the pub where she used to sing and the nearby Chinese takeaway.

How different was the life Susan was now leading. Virtually anything that she wanted she got. As well as the household staff there was a BMW with blacked-out windows at her disposal, with driver.

Although the car had state-of-the-art interior with air-conditioning, it was never put on in case it damaged Susan's voice. She'd also been given membership of the local gym, and advice on which foods she should eat.

Whenever Susan went out she could have her own security guard alongside her. There were also reports that her teeth had been whitened – especially important for the Americans – and that her eyebrows, once so bushy, were trimmed regularly. She also had, naturally, a complete new wardrobe.

Susan was also by now provided with a credit card and a financial adviser. She and Simon Cowell were said to speak to each other at least twice a week and she was one of the select band of intimates who had his secret second mobile phone number.

Asked about Scotland, Susan had told *Harpers*, 'I'll go back to visit, but you have to move on.' But spokesman for her said, 'People are saying that she has turned her back on Scotland but that is not true at all. She is down in London for the time being, as she is working here, and you can imagine what the commute would be like. She is planning to go back for visits and wants to buy the house she lived in.'

The regulars at the Happy Valley Hotel said that they were thrilled by her transformation, and wished her luck. Her local councillor, Jim Swan, added, 'She looks fantastic.'

Brother Gerry said, 'Susan loves the life she is leading

now, but it has left her fearful of going back to how things were, living on her own waiting for her singing dream to come true.' He also said that that she just could not bear it if people didn't like her.

'Susan doesn't take rejection well. It's a lack of confidence.'

In the middle of a great deal of conjecture as to whether Susan had, albeit inadvertently, turned her back on Scotland, she went on holiday in August – to Blackburn. She could have gone anywhere in the world, instead she returned to her home town – where it rained throughout her stay. She didn't head for Edinburgh's fine dining restaurants either, preferring to go out to her favourite fish and chip takeaway, Valentes in Bathgate.

A friend said, 'As soon as she got some time off, there was never any chance Susan would head for St Tropez or Barbados. She was always going home to Blackburn. It is the place where she feels happiest and most at ease.'

With her assistant and chaperone Ciaran Doig, she slipped home practically unnoticed for her break and rather than head for a plush hotel she stayed in her semi-detached council house. She spent time reading the scores of letters that had landed on her doormat from fans across the globe and on Sunday attended morning mass at Our Lady of Lourdes church, where she used to work as a volunteer.

Dressed in a new coat and cashmere scarf, she looked happy, relaxed and brimming with confidence as she arrived at the church and chatted with friends. Her styled brown hair and bright outfit were a world away from her pre-fame shock of wild grey locks and dowdy gear, but she was nowhere near as elegant as she had been for the *Harpers* shoot.

She was met by an autograph-hunter as she made her way into church but managed to go on a shopping trip to Bathgate and relax with friends over a glass of lemonade at the Happy Valley.

The friend added, 'Susan loves London and is enjoying being treated like a superstar while she follows her dream of becoming a singer. But she's spent her entire life in Blackburn and was overjoyed at getting the chance to come home and be normal again. She's a regular at morning Mass at the church and loved getting back into the old routine.

'This holiday has been perfect in allowing Susan to switch off from the demands of recording and she loved catching up with friends and family. The only thing missing was sunshine.'

No sooner had Susan's break finished than she discovered that her debut album was number one in the charts – months ahead of its release. It topped the Amazon pre-order chart even though *I Dreamed A Dream* would not be on sale until 23 November; tens of thousands of copies had already been sold to fans placing early orders on the shopping website.

The CD was even outselling Whitney Houston's

comeback album, as well as other pre-release titles such as the *Twilight* soundtrack.

As well as 'Cry Me A River', the album also contained a cover version of Madonna's 1995 hit 'You'll See', at Susan's insistence.

'It's a song she has loved for years. She sang it at auditions for TV shows and music contests when she used to be cruelly turned away by people. At the end, when she was sometimes reduced to tears, she used to say "You'll see". And she's proof she can do it now as one of the most famous women in the world,' said a source.

If a combination of Madonna and Susan seemed strange, it was no less weird than 'Susan sings The Rolling Stones'.

'Wild Horses' was from the Stones' classic album *Sticky Fingers*. A slow, mournful tune, it is the opposite of the storming rock songs that made them famous. It also happened to be Jagger's former wife Jerry Hall's favourite song by the band and had previously been covered by Neil Young, Garbage, Deacon Blue and The Cranberries among others.

Susan summed up her feelings for the song: 'How could you help but be drawn in by this haunting theme? It conjures up memories of childhood amongst Council Estates, poverty and struggle in the first verse. Irony and bitterness – one of my personal favourites and an emotional release.'

Her first public performance of the song was to be in

the land that had taken her to its heart, America. And when she landed all hell broke loose. On the second Saturday of September, thousands of fans turned out to welcome her into the country, her first visit there.

She was greeted at Los Angeles Airport by cheering admirers and more than 50 paparazzi and numerous camera teams. Screaming well-wishers clamoured to get a glimpse of her, in scenes normally reserved for Hollywood A-listers.

Looking confident and relaxed, SuBo smiled at the crowds and blew kisses before waving for the cameras, but the crowd was so great that she needed two minders to pave her way through the throng. It took more than five minutes for her to reach her waiting car and the crowd were chanting, 'Susan, Susan' as they surrounded her.

There were also cries of 'We love you Susan!' and one young fan got close enough to hug the singer amid the scrum.

Susan met with record company executives at the Hotel Bel-Air and had tea with them – she was astonished to see that the bill for the refreshments came to £300! Once she had rested, the next stop was Disneyland – it had been her dream since childhood to go there – where she looked a little apprehensive as she rode around on Dumbo, although she perked up in time to make waves on Disneyland's Splash Mountain attraction as yet more adoring US fans clamoured to catch a glimpse of their hero.

The wonderful world of Disney was not the real reason that she had crossed the Atlantic. No, the main purpose was to perform 'Wild Horses' on *America's Got Talent*. It would be a wonderful platform for the song, and if it did succeed and make it to number one in America. Susan would be following in the footsteps of the teenage Lulu who reached the top with 'To Sir, With Love' in 1967. Fellow Scot Lulu, now 60, was a fan of Susan's too, announcing she had 'a rare wee voice'.

One of the most amazing aspects of Susan's rise to fame had been the way that she had appealed to millions of Americans. With an attraction that was perhaps even greater than in the UK, Stateside she was massive. There was something in her that appealed to admirers 'across the pond'. She was the embodiment of the 'American Dream', the hope that you really can get from a log cabin to the White House. Susan was born on the wrong side of the tracks, she had no friends in high places, she didn't look like a movie star – but she'd made it all the same. She had a voice and that talent was enough to make her successful. And unlike in the UK, where the cheers seemed to turn to sneers very quickly – remember those who booed at the *Britain's Got Talent* final and at her live appearances? – in America, success was applauded. They didn't build you up to shoot you down; they built you up to admire you. And people thought, 'If she can do it, so can I. And if I can't do it, then maybe my kids can.' Perhaps it was this aspect of the SuBo phenomenon that attracted them.

Piers Morgan, who was a judge on the American show as well as the British one, said, 'If she's up for it and she is well enough then our feeling is she probably will – absolutely. Susan singing live to 25 million Americans? That would be great.'

Morgan added, 'She still gets a bit tired sometimes, but she is 48.'

'We didn't want to fall into the trap of looking at every middle-aged woman as the next Susan Boyle. That would be pointless. With Susan, it was a moment of total surprise and electricity. There's no denying that everyone wants to see if we have our own Susan Boyle,' said the American show's executive producer, Cécile Frot-Coutaz. 'The worst thing we could do is find our own version. The more you try to engineer it, the less you achieve on the desired outcome.'

Paul Telegdy, chief of reality programming at NBC, the channel that broadcast *America's Got Talent*, said the show expected Boyle's meteoric rise from obscurity to provide a ratings boost to *AGT*, which for the past two years had been massively popular throughout the summer.

Her sudden fame would be 'very effective in letting the public know that this is what *America's Got Talent* is about: a democracy for any act, age range or personal story,' Frot-Coutaz said.

Susan had already had an effect on the show, even though she had never been on it, thanks to her YouTube hit and the massive attention it attracted in America.

'We definitely saw a lot more people coming to audition who'd been told they would never make it, either because of their look or they didn't fit the mould,' said host Nick Cannon. 'People felt if [Boyle] can do it, they can.'

US public relations expert Steve Jaffe, who had worked with former president Bill Clinton and film star Leonardo DiCaprio, put her success down to her 'underdog' image. 'Susan Boyle is the classic example of what Americans want in their entertainment and in their lives. She represents hope. Americans dine on hope,' he said.

'Susan Boyle's an underdog – a real rags to riches tale. That's why we idolise people who are stars and that's in large part what motivates us. We dream a dream that we can be like Susan Boyle. She's the real thing, the genuine article, and we all believe that if she can make it, we can make it.'

He added, 'Susan is someone who is without pretence. Americans grow up knowing that there's an American Dream out there for them if they really try. Susan Boyle waited for her big break and grabbed it. No one expected her to be at such a professional level when she first appeared. We judged her by her plain appearance but she had heart. That's why we have embraced her – Susan sings from the heart.'

Even as the crowds were welcoming her into LAX Airport, Lulu was pointing out, 'It is hard to say if Susan Boyle mania is justified. It's amazing. It steps over into celebrity and that is hard to deal with. In a way, it would be better to just let her sing her song and go home. But you have to take both. I just hope she is going to be able to handle it because it's not easy. Everyone can trip up and have their hiccups, but it is about how you recover. When I found fame, it was very exciting and scary at the same time. I was carried off in a whirlwind. I had a very nice manager who was a mother figure, so I was fortunate. It's hard to do the work if you don't have the right people around you.'

If there were any doubts that America's love affair with Susan might end in tears, they were dispelled that evening. An estimated 25 million people – the largest audience of the night – tuned in to hear her sing. She was a sensation.

America's Got Talent host Nick Cannon called her 'a singer who took the whole world by storm just a few short months ago. She was launched on an extraordinary journey to take her to unprecedented global fame overnight.'

Backed by a pianist, a string section and a tuxedo-clad choir, Susan appeared in a black gown, with her hair straightened, and was given a standing ovation by the studio audience and judges, who included Sharon Osbourne and Piers Morgan.

'Wow, truly amazing,' Cannon said after her performance.

Speaking on the show, Susan referred to the loss of her

mother. 'I was very lonely to begin with. The loneliness really kicked in. I found myself crying a lot. I found I couldn't manage or cope. But I know she meant me to do something with my life.'

She also talked about her spell in the Priory clinic after the pressure became too much following the *BGT* final. 'I don't remember much about it after the final. All I remember is being put in an ambulance and taken to this clinic. I've never felt so tired. I look back on it now and it was a necessity because I was tired. I don't know what was wrong with me though. I used to be a spectator looking out at the world and now I am part of that world and, although frightening, I want to embrace it because I feel a bit more confident within myself right now, more able to cope, more able to take part in the dream. I'm ready to get there and get on with it now. I'm not the wee frightened wee lassie I used to be.'

The contest, incidentally, was won by country singer Kevin Skinner, a chicken farmer, who received one million dollars and a headline slot in Las Vegas and was understandably reduced to tears by his victory.

As well as that massive audience, Susan attracted rave reviews from the American media. Perhaps the most noteworthy of these came from the pop music critic of the *Los Angeles Times*. 'Susan Boyle placed her hands on her abdomen as she sang the last note of the song "Wild Horses" Wednesday on the finale of *America's Got Talent*, taking the familiar stance of a trained singer, carefully locating her breath. The pose concluded a performance that was exactly what Boyle's mentor, Simon Cowell, could have hoped for – lovely, inspirational, free of surprises.

'Devotees of the original Rolling Stones version of this often-covered weeper might object to Boyle's stolid rhythmic sense, her utter lack of irony (irony is, after all, the essence of Mick Jagger), and her artistic choices, which transform "Wild Horses" from a complicated account of emotional confusion to a simple exclamation of longing. But mainstream America, at least as it's portrayed on prime-time television, adores Boyle's sunny vocal tone and her ability to turn even a song about a drug overdose into something worthy of church.'

The article went on to point out that her performance was canned (it was taped the night before the telecast, though made to look live) and that her nerves clearly planted her to one spot, but that it didn't matter. It continued:

'Ever since she appeared on *Britain's Got Talent*, the UK version of this global talent-show franchise, Boyle has become one of the world's most celebrated regular people. Working class, average looking and too old even to join the cast of *Desperate Housewives*, Boyle inspired many by pursuing her dream of becoming a professional in a field, entertainment, that mostly rewards the young and the beautiful.

'She's not the first star to defy beauty standards: there was Ethel Merman, Janis Joplin, heck, even *American Idol* had the chubby Christian rocker Chris Sligh. Perhaps because her voice is so pure while her chin is so wobbly, Boyle seems truly exceptional.'

The report continued by saying that the public were behind Susan for reasons that had nothing to do with the way she sings. 'It is heartening to see a not-quite-50-year-old woman who'd never previously caught a break find success, even if at times she seems more traumatised than fulfilled by fame. But to be surprised by her singing is, frankly, an unfair response. Boyle has trained hard to sing the way she does; she is as careful as a singer comes. We should stop being startled by her performances and respect her for the qualities she's cultivated: scrupulousness and dependability.

'At 48, Boyle is old enough to have been a teen fan of the Rolling Stones. Perhaps the spunkiness that helped make her famous led her to choose a chestnut by those bad boys as the single from her debut album, to be released Nov. 24. Her rise has given the pop world an interesting new personality and music lovers a chance to embrace yet another very pretty voice.'

If that astonishing assessment of her performance was not enough, there were many more who echoed its sentiments. Eric Ditzian, of MTV, said she brought the house down; the *Examiner* called her performance 'subdued yet elegant'; while one of the world's most influential blogs, the *Huffington Post*, said she had arguably 'stolen the show'.

David Hinckley of the *New York Daily News* commented: 'She did it mostly with piano accompaniment, in a deliberate style that sounded at times like a soaring theatrical ballad and other times like something out of a hymnal.

'It definitely wasn't rock 'n' roll – which is good, because that would have been just too bizarre. But it was still a bold choice from a woman who said in interviews that show tunes were her music.

'She sang the song confidently, even when some of the lyrics seemed disconnected from any personal experience – and it certainly wasn't the oddest Rolling Stones song she could have chosen.'

Amanda Holden, who was in America at the time, was interviewed on CBS News shortly after the broadcast.

'I cannot it tell you how proud I was. My mother was out with me at the moment and we were both sat there, here in Nashville, watching her being embraced by America. I thought it was the most self-assured, confident performance I've ever seen her do. And I think that it's really showing now in her personality, the love that she's been shown… It was beautiful, really beautiful. It blew me away. I think it was the best thing she's done so far. I have to say that I heard the song two weeks ago. Simon gave us a sneak listen. It was me and

Simon and Piers at Simon's house in Los Angeles. It was very dark. Simon has fires all around his swimming pool and he said listen to this, and he put the CD on.

And we listened and it was – her voice just rang out into the darkness and it was the most ethereal kind of spiritual moment ever. I thought even Simon was going to cry. I mean he couldn't believe it. I think she sounds like a cross between kind of Kate Bush and Barbra Streisand at the moment. Her voice quality is stunning. I mean and that song choice is genius, just genius. I think that she's found the middle ground. Her hair looks lovely. She didn't have too much makeup on. She's got a very pretty face. And I think that the makeup she had on last night kind of just accentuated that in a – in a very subtle kind of way. And I also thought she looked lovely, she was kind of very regal. I loved how she thanked the orchestra afterwards. She was very centred, very calm. It's just brilliant.'

Holden also revealed how knowing Susan was now getting her into places she might otherwise have struggled to enter. 'To get into places, whenever they asked, "Who is it for?" I'd say, "Do you know Susan Boyle? I'm the judge on that show."

'They would be like, "Oh my gaawwd! Wow, Susan Boyle!" And we would be in.

'It's amazing – she seems to have reached every corner of the world. I don't think she realises her fame is growing. Susan has been in a little bubble in LA, making her album, and probably thinks the world has forgotten about her.'

The world certainly hadn't forgotten about Susan. She got a rapturous ovation from fellow fans of her beloved Celtic when she performed the half-time draw on the pitch at their Parkhead ground during a European clash with Hamburg at the end of October and, as the excitement grew nearing the release of her CD, she came out with an astonishing admission: Susan, the 48-year-old spinster who 'had never been kissed' let alone anything else, had once been near to marriage.

She was quoted in the *Sun* newspaper as saying, 'I had a boyfriend, John. He asked me to marry him, but he got cold feet. We had only ever had a peck on the cheek.

'I just thought, "I don't think so. We're not getting married after just a few weeks." He got cold feet. It made me sad, in a way. You feel unattractive. You feel life is passing you by.'

She also said how shocked she was by her 'wee wifey' appearance when she first saw herself on television. 'I saw this wee wifey with the mad hairdo and the bushy eyebrows and said, "Hmmm, not really telegenic".'

As always with fame, however, there were downsides. Susan's loss of privacy was hard to cope with for a woman who had lived such an anonymous, mundane existence for so long. The press and a posse of photographers were continually around her, looking for snippets here a revealing photograph there. There was another kind of follower too, people of a more disturbing nature. By mid-November she had been given extra security after a crazed stalker turned up at her home in Blackburn.

Susan had been bombarded with weird letters from the middle-aged American woman after her initial YouTube appearance. The stalker then arrived unannounced in Blackburn and although a bodyguard intercepted her, when Simon Cowell heard of the incident, which left Susan 'shaken up', he ordered increased protection for her.

The incident was especially disturbing because at a London book signing a few weeks earlier *The X Factor* winner Leona Lewis had been punched by a deranged fan.

'This woman is constantly following Susan around the world,' a friend revealed. 'It is a middle-aged American woman who has become obsessed with her. At first, people thought it was no more than a nuisance. But after what happened to Leona everyone is taking extra precautions. This is an important month for Susan and everyone wants it to go smoothly.'

With the release date for her album approaching, an Edinburgh-based security firm was hired to protect her, although Susan seemed to be unperturbed by the danger, said friends.

She was even out on her doorstep in a polka-dot dressing gown waving to neighbours and giving them the thumbs-up. For luck she added a typical hip-wiggle and, in anticipation of the success of the album, said, 'Things are great. It will be an absolute honour to be No. 1.'

In the run-up to the CD release, Susan gave an interview to the *Daily Mirror* in which she revealed more of the troubled life she had led as a child – she had been hit with a belt every day by brutal teachers and cruelly taunted by other children – and the impact it had had on her in the ensuing years. One of the blackest periods of her life, she told the paper, was when she was bullied at school. 'There's nothing worse than another person having power over you by bullying you and you not knowing how to get rid of that thing.

'After mum died it didn't fully register until maybe six months after. That's when the loneliness set in and there was nobody around except my cat Pebbles. When you lose someone as powerful as your mum you feel as if a part of you is taken away and that does things to your confidence.'

She said music was 'a complete emotional release' from the problems she encountered in her youth, explaining, 'This feels like a good way of making up for that – a very, very enjoyable way of making up for it as well.'

That wasn't, of course, the only interview that Susan gave. In contrast to the anodyne conversation she had with American television, she was remarkably candid in a talk with Ian 'Molly' Meldrum for Australian television. His down-to-earth, low-key questioning allowed her to reveal much more of the torment she had been through at various stages in her life, than the fairly saccharin approach of interviewing in the US.

She expanded on the points he had raised in the *Mirror*: 'When people are a wee bit slow, others pick at them,' she said. 'My life was made absolute hell.' She said she was constantly 'made a fool of' at school, and admitted that the jibes have left her emotionally scarred and holding on to a lot of anger.

'I can be up and down like a yo-yo. I can be depressed. I can be a bit funny after being tired, but when I go on stage I forget all about that. I feel I've got a communication with the audience. I'm told I'm a different person on stage.

'I know I'm taking a big chance telling people this, but you have to be honest. I used to be made a fool of at school. It was psychological bullying and that leaves a scar and it also cultivates a lot of anger.'

When Meldrum pointed out that she had given hope to others with her success, she took up his theme by saying, 'Especially those who tend to be the underdog like myself. I have a slight disability and people have always been saying to me "you can't do this and you can't do that, or you can't take this job" or whatever. It made me so annoyed and angry and frustrated. I like to think that people who dare to dream a dream can have that dream come true through their own determination.

'So when I went on *Britain's Got Talent* it was a chance to prove myself. I had a lot of friends in the community who said I had a reasonable voice and obviously I had the support of my mother and members of my family, which is very important.

'In some ways I had a conflict with my mother. Everybody argues, everybody does things they should not do. And it was really was poignant and it did make me cry, and I'm trying not to do that now, that she is not alive to see how proud I would have made her. I know she would have been proud of me.'

When Meldrum pointed out her success around the world, her response was simple: 'All I did was open my gob and sing. I just made a noise. Everybody does it you know…'

Was the pressure too great? 'Pressure is good because it makes you work hard, but it works against you when you get a bit tired, you need rest periods in between. That's the only way I can handle it. But other than that it's been good fun.'

She added, 'If people didn't recognise you I might end up saying, "What am I doing wrong?"

'Everybody goes through phases where they think should I give up and if I hadn't made that promise to my mother then I probably would have given up… I did not have a path in life. I did not have anything set out for me. A lot of people have their lives mapped out for them, mine was not. I did not know what I wanted to be. I did not know what I was good at. I wasn't told I was good at anything. I was always kept down. So the question there was what was I going to be, what was my goal, what was my place in life.'

It was a remarkable interview by the grizzled Aussie, who had coaxed more out of Susan than anyone before.

It wasn't all doom and gloom, though, Susan was quite perky throughout it too, and at one stage when Meldrum asked her jokingly if she would replace Mick Jagger in the Stones for a version of 'Wild Horses', she reduced him to laughter with an impromptu impersonation of the Stones' singer.

Although 'SuBo mania' was still as strong as ever, and there had been the rendition of 'Wild Horses' in the US, Susan had not sung in public or on-screen in the UK for some time. Therefore, a story about her singing 'Wild Horses' on the *The X Factor* at the time of her album release towards the end of November was billed as ' a comeback'!

It would be the first time she had been back to Fountain Studios in Wembley – the original home of many classic TV programmes such as *Ready, Steady, Go* and *No Hiding Place* and where she had lost out in the *BGT* final to Diversity.

It was a wonderful return to the stage for Susan, who received a standing ovation from the audience before she'd even sung a note. She said it was 'bloody great' to be back, and added, 'I feel at home and I loved performing. The public should watch out for the album.'

Simon Cowell told her, 'I feel so proud of you and it's lovely to have you here.'

She was struggling with a cold and needed two 'takes' to get 'Wild Horses' right as she coughed during the first version of the song. Fortunately it was pre-recorded so when it was transmitted the rendition was described as 'flawless' by critics. The *Daily Mirror* said she had 'made a triumphant return to British TV.' Pop diva Mariah Carey had also pre-recorded her number for the show, and for the same reason as Susan – being double-booked. Susan had to fly to America on the day the *The X Factor* was being televised in order to plug the new album and it was impossible for her to be in two places at once.

Reuters News Agency circulated a story that weekend which summed up the fever-pitch feeling as the minutes ticked by until the official release of Susan's album:

'Scottish singer Susan Boyle, one of the biggest stars of the Internet age, seeks to turn global celebrity into record sales next week with the release of her debut album *I Dreamed a Dream*.

'Named after the song from the musical *Les Misérables* that made her famous, the 12-track album is a mix of pop covers like Madonna's "You'll See" and The Monkees' "Daydream Believer" and Christian stalwarts like "Amazing Grace" and "Silent Night".

'The Sony Music record hits stores in Britain on

Monday and in the United States on Tuesday, and the early commercial signs are promising.

'The album is the largest ever global CD pre-order on online retailer Amazon.com, with sales reportedly in excess of 100,000, and is the bookmakers' favourite to top the British chart over the lucrative Christmas period.'

The story did end with a rare downbeat note, however, when it added: 'Early reviews have been unfavourable... with *The Times* newspaper calling it "an uncomfortable package" in a two-out-of-five star review, the same rating as the *Guardian*.'

If that was a slightly downbeat end to the item, the same could not be said of many of the other reviews. The *Scotsman*, for example, said: '*I Dreamed A Dream* has become the most pre-ordered album of all time and her unexpectedly accomplished version of The Rolling Stones' "Wild Horses" is ubiquitous. The camera may not have loved her on her initial TV appearance but, on this evidence, the recording studio does seem to. *I Dreamed A Dream* is certainly better than it needed to be for such a sure commercial thing, with some thought invested in the song selection.' The review continued by saying that Susan 'tests her chops on the seminal "Cry Me a River", revealing classiness, sassiness and an understanding of phrasing along the way; and displays some devotional fervour on Patty Griffin's gospely "Up To the Mountain", inspired by Martin Luther King's "I've been to the mountaintop speech".'

Julian Monaghan, head of music buying at Amazon.co.uk, said, 'Just eight months ago, no one was aware of the talents of Susan Boyle. Now, she has generated more Amazon pre-order CD sales globally than any artist. That is an incredible achievement and is testament to the fact that she has captured the hearts of people all over Britain, America and the rest of the world.'

Susan had been to the US before, for that appearance in Los Angeles, but now New York was in her sights as she flew out to promote the album. She was welcomed by a crowd of fans straining at the barriers at JFK airport, some of whom were waving pictures of her, others tartan banners and Scotland flags or posters declaring their love for her. No wonder Susan was moved to say:

'It was really knockout actually. Especially at the airports. It's quite a lot to take in and it's a bit overwhelming at times – I've got to be honest here.'

Many of the admirers who came to greet her at JFK were middle-aged women – one of her core groups of fans – and they wore red scarves similar to the ones Susan had been seen in as a gesture of solidarity with her. One internet fan site alone had 37,000 registered fans – and the number was rising by the day. Interestingly, as well as Susan's much-discussed appearance and voice, her religious faith was also said to be one of the reasons Americans had such an affinity with her.

She was to sing three songs from the album. Wrapped

up tight a cold New York wind, Susan sang 'Wild Horses' plus 'Cry Me a River' and 'I Dreamed a Dream' on an outdoor stage at the Rockefeller Plaza for millions watching on television.

Interviewed by *Today* presenter Matt Lauer, Boyle said she had changed since that first performance which became the massive YouTube hit.

'I've grown up a bit,' she said. 'I've become more of a lady. I don't swivel my hips as much, you know?'

She added that one of the songs on her album, the cover of Madonna's 'You'll See', was her answer to those who she says bullied her at school. 'That was a statement I was trying to make, because I was bullied a lot at school: "You may have done that to me when I was younger, but you can't do it to me any more. I'm grown up now."'

She was backed by an orchestra and hundreds of fans – many who had travelled across the country to see her – surrounded her as, at one point, she whooped loudly and waved her scarf in the air.

The whistle-stop visit was not without incident, however. At one stage Susan sucked her thumb and was apparently staring into the distance. And, finally, she burst into tears with her head in her hands. It happened after she was given a patchwork quilt that had been stitched together by hundreds of people, from 28 countries including the UK, USA, Australia, Canada, Mexico, Poland, Japan and Antarctica.

One source said, 'Everyone around her is acutely aware how susceptible she is to becoming emotional when under stress. She has just undertaken a tour of America, which would put anyone under enormous pressure.

'It seems to have taken its toll and she was upset. She is being closely monitored and given all the support she needs.'

A spokesman for Susan played down the incident, saying, 'She was just overjoyed and extremely touched with the reception she has had from everyone in America.'

Afterwards she went up the Empire State Building to film some footage for an ITV special due to go out mid-December. And the next day she was taken to CBS for a pre-recorded interview and performance. She then went for lunch to the Tavern on the Green with her entourage – her publicist, personal assistant, record company executives and bodyguards.

By the end of the week Susan was back home in Blackburn. She had swapped the luxury of her £2,800-a night suite at the Ritz-Carlton, with its French linen bedding and yellow chintz furniture, for the place she really called home.

Back behind the mock-Georgian white door of her pebble-dash council home she was said to be making plans to leave her London flat and relinquish her gym membership and chauffer-driven car. She was swapping the granite kitchen and cream walls of that luxury apartment for a pair of well-used beige velour armchairs, a collection of brass teapots on the fireplace and a dusty whisky jar filled with loose change.

One of her public relations team said, 'Home is the one in Blackburn that she grew up in, and that is the home she wants to live in. She will not be buying a house in London. Her London pad, which is rented, is convenient for the time being. Because of Susan being in London to work on the album she has been splitting her time, but she will be back in Scotland very soon, with Pebbles.'

Those thumb-sucking pictures and the tears in New York had led some observers to speculate that Susan was on the brink again, but she denied this once she had settled in back home. She said that one the fans had asked her how her career was progressing and she replied she was taking things slowly and progressing in 'baby steps' and put her thumb in her mouth as a joke. She couldn't believe it when photographs of the incident were later accompanied by text suggesting she could be having a breakdown.

The tears were simply that she was moved by the caring nature of her admirers who had taken so much trouble to make her a quilt. 'I'm happy and doing fine. I have never been accepted by the world before. Now I do feel part of it and I find it really exciting. I feel very content within myself, and as I'm finally achieving my dream I feel so lucky and privileged. I keep asking myself, "Is this really happening?" And I keep expecting someone to say, "Ha ha, love, we're kidding."' She insisted she was loving being famous, saying, 'Everyone has fears but mine is probably that this will all disappear. I want it to keep on going as long as possible. If it did all go away tomorrow, I know that I've enjoyed every moment of living the dream now.'

The acceptance that she was now receiving was the best aspect of her fame, she felt, after being taunted in her childhood. 'It means I'm a wee bit slower at picking things up than other people. But I've got a great deal more ability than people give me credit for. At school, I felt very frustrated, very lonely – people didn't want to sit next to me in class. I was often bawling my eyes out and it does tend to chip away at your personality.'

And as for her new appearance: 'I keep reading that I've had all this Botox, the teeth whitening... but I haven't had that at all. I've been working hard and lost a bit of weight which has been good for me. The whole process has been good for me.'

By that final weekend of November 2009, 700,000 copies of Susan's album had been sold in one week in the US alone. In Britain it was an estimated 400,000.

'I went to LA and there were great crowds waiting for us at the airport,' she said. 'It was quite something – nothing that a woman like me was used to, for heaven's sake. But I found Americans to be incredibly warm and friendly.

'It was quite something to be in Hollywood. The hotel I was staying in, apparently Frank Sinatra used to take his women there. And I dipped my toes in the same pool Grace Kelly had been in.

'This is a world I'd never seen before and never dreamt that I would get to see. I can't wait to visit again.'

She repeated the fact that her one regret was that her parents were not alive to see her amazing transformation. Her father Patrick, a miner and pub singer, had died ten years earlier.

'I think they would be very proud of me – I hope they would. I've done a lot of wrong with my parents. There's no one around that hasn't. But hopefully I've made up for that now and they're smiling down on me. I can feel it sometimes. The only dream my dad had, of becoming a singer, is coming true through me – so I think he'd be proud!'

Brother Gerry had his views on Susan and the remarkable situation she was in, global superstar on one hand, middle-aged spinster in a council house on the other.

'I worry Susan will become totally consumed by fame and lose touch with reality,' he revealed. 'If that happens the lid could come off at any moment. I need to protect her because she is still so insecure and vulnerable. Her family is her only anchor. Without us she could be cut adrift.

'Susan said she was in great spirits but it was clear she had become totally overwhelmed by the reaction to her by the American public. I kept asking her, "Are you calm, are you happy?" and Susan replied that she's where she wants to be, which reassured me. I told Susan she needed to kick back quietly for a few days and spent time carefully telling her everyone loved her especially her family and of course her beloved cat Pebbles, which she always asks about.'

What worried him, he said, is that Susan was aware she can be the hottest thing around today and be gone tomorrow.

'She talks to me regularly and calls at bizarre hours of the day and night. Immediately I have to bring her back down to earth doing the old brother-and-sister chat. Susan's so huge but she is still coming to terms with it all even six months or so down the road. She pours out her heart to me all the time and can get into a groove of feeling sorry for herself. I spoke to Susan before she flew out to America and she knew this was really the start of the big time. But that also brings its problems if her head isn't in the right place. She is so different to everyone else and the least thing can send her into a pit of depression.

'It's a phenomenon to Susan and what I do, deliberately, is let her talk about her career for a minute and then suddenly change the subject and inject a bit of normality. It's the way forward for Susan,' he told the *People* newspaper.

'From June she's been rocking up on TV all over the world and become a prisoner in her own home and hotel room.

'She has an excellent management team but I'm there

for her emotional support. Of course the money is great for Susan, but she is happiest sitting at home by the fire with Pebbles.

'I know Susan would give up the millions just to stay happy and normal.

'The Priory was good for her but the battle against depression and stress is a day-to-day fight. In a strange way the more she is loved the more worried she becomes.'

Gerry added, 'Simon Cowell has been a great support to Susan... But don't forget Susan put herself up for the show – no one else. What Susan needs is a few days sitting alongside her fire with her phone off and Pebbles purring on her lap.'

The experienced publicist Max Clifford, who represented Simon Cowell, had his own verdict on the best way of helping Susan. 'Back in the Sixties, we had The Beatles and that was astronomical. But it still took weeks and months for them to gain worldwide fame. For Susan, it was literally minutes. There's never been anything quite like this before. She will have people there keeping an eye on her, protecting her from excess and her new band of over-enthusiastic admirers.

'The important thing is to let her do it her way and then, in a few weeks or months, she might say "I can't do this anymore" – but she has to make that decision. I think everyone has been taken a bit by surprise. Nobody in the industry has worked with a Susan Boyle before.

'But they have learned and adjusted and Simon Cowell

has made sure that her family is kept very close and everything is done the way that is comfortable for her.

'There's a very good chance she will be around for a while because she has a lovely voice and a wonderful story that has captured the hearts of millions. But she is the most unlikely star I think we'll ever see.'

Susan's record sales were astounding. When the official figures were released, in its first week in the UK the album sold 410,000 – the best first week figure for an album since records began. She took the record for the best first week's sale for a debut album from another reality TV star – *The X Factor* winner Leona Lewis whose album, *Spirit*, sold more than 375,000 copies in its first week in November 2007.

She in turn had beaten the previous record set by the Arctic Monkeys in 2006 for their debut *Whatever People Say I Am, That's What I'm Not*.

Martin Talbot, of the Official Charts Company, said: 'Susan Boyle's achievement is quite phenomenal. After all of the excitement surrounding her appearance on *Britain's Got Talent*, everyone expected her to make a big impact when she released her first music. But to arrive with such a bang is exceptional.'

It was a similar story in the States where the album soared to No. 1 in the US charts. Her CD sold a record 701,000 copies in its first week across the Atlantic – over three times that of nearest rival, Italian tenor Andrea Bocelli.

That meant it was the fastest-selling female debut album ever – with two million copies shifted worldwide. In the States, her CD was the fastest selling by a female artist ever. Only US male rapper Snoop Dogg had sold more in a debut week. The album was also No. 1 in Ireland, Australia, New Zealand and Canada and many other countries around the world.

Simon Cowell said, 'She's like a great underdog story – it's like a Hollywood movie. It's this lonely lady living in her little house in this little village in Scotland who for all her life had dreamt of becoming a star.

'Nobody had ever taken her seriously and her last attempt was to come on *Britain's Got Talent*. The minute she starts singing her life changes forever.

'I'm incredibly proud of Susan as well as being delighted for her,' he said. 'The success could not have happened to a lovelier person. She did it her way and made a dream come true. In *Britain's Got Talent*, she opened her mouth and the world fell in love with her, which is why her album has been the fastest-selling of anyone making their debut.'

Such was Susan's fame by now that the smallest remark by her was likely to be given space in the newspapers and on websites. So when she said meeting *Baywatch* star David Hasselhoff, now one of the judges on *America's Got Talent*, was one of the highlights of her rise to fame, the news travelled around the world. 'The most memorable moment has been on *America's*

Got Talent when I met Piers, Sharon Osbourne and The Hoff – he's a nice wee hunk,' Susan quipped.

The favour had been repaid by 'The Hoff', who had said Susan was responsible for 'bringing the world together.'

In one radio interview she said, as an aside, that when she died she would like to have the children's song 'Nellie The Elephant' by Mandy Miller played at her funeral. That news too spread like wildfire.

Amid all this frenzy, it is interesting to analysis what a fellow singer thought of her. Bette Midler – the Divine Miss M – had been at the top of the tree for three decades and so was in a unique position to comment on both Susan and her success. Being Midler, she would not come out with platitudes either; she wasn't that kind person.

'I think the choice of material is very bright because a lot of it is faith-based and there is a large part of the population who are attracted to the church. She is an act whose time has come,' said the star. 'People love that kind of voice. She sings straight. She does not do a lot of riffing. There are no trills, no thrills. It's straight singing and it comes from the heart.'

CHAPTER THIRTEEN

THE WORLD
AT HER FEET

Piers Morgan looked straight at the camera and announced: 'Together for the very first time... please welcome Elaine Paige and Susan Boyle!'

It was the evening of 13 December 2009, just eight months after that *Britain's Got Talent* audition in Glasgow had been screened, and Susan Boyle's world had changed forever.

At the audition, there had been laughter and eyebrows raised in surprise that this unknown woman had even dared to mention her wish to emulate Elaine Paige. Yet here they were, about to share a stage together. And it was on a show devoted to Susan, not Elaine Paige!

Morgan was right; it was the first and long-awaited teaming of the two – one an iconic figure, a living-legend of the musical stage, the other a woman who had brought a new meaning to the phrase ' Showbiz Sensation'.

From the first moment Susan had captured the

imagination of the world, Paige had expressed an interest in singing with her. And now, at last, it was to happen. The song they were to sing was 'I Know Him So Well', a number that Paige had had a massive hit with years before when she recorded it with Barbara Dickson.

From the musical *Chess*, the song had a superb pedigree. Not only were Paige and Dickson two of the most respected women singers in the business, the number was written by Tim Rice and the Abba pair Benny Andersson and Björn Ulvaeus, men with impeccable track-records of creating popular music masterpieces. Many stars had performed it in the past, including Barbra Streisand and Whitney Houston, and it had even been the subject of a merciless spoof by comediennes Dawn French and Jennifer Saunders.

This was no tongue-in-cheek approach, of course, as Elaine Paige, looking stunning on television that Sunday evening in a shimmering blue dress, began singing the opening verse of the bittersweet song, a dialogue between the estranged wife and the mistress of a chess champion. As Susan, looking chic in a full-length rich-brown dress, began to take part in the song and walked across the stage to join her, the audience at the London Studios applauded instinctively. For over three minutes the pair harmonised, the song's Abba roots showing strongly, and when it ended they embraced each other. As Susan looked downwards, Paige whispered comfortingly in her ear as the audience cheered. Susan blew her a little kiss.

Piers Morgan was moved to say, 'I am not actually sure who was the most excited there, but it was probably me.'

Susan sang two other solo songs, 'Who I Was Born To Be' and ' Cry Me A River' that evening, before finishing, inevitably, with 'I Dreamed A Dream'. Unlike that day in Glasgow a lifetime earlier, she was not alone on stage this time. Around her she had the cast from *Les Misérables* and there she stood, centre-stage of this massive production, the centrepiece of the most successful musical of all time.

Ten million viewers tuned in to watch the hour-long special on ITV and when the show aired in the US, on the TV Guide Network, it became the highest rated television special in its history.

Given the millions of words that had been written about her and the countless hours of radio and television air time she'd had, it seemed unlikely that there would be anything new that could be said about her. Nevertheless, there was some intriguing information aired that night about how she had been received and perceived that day in Glasgow.

Declan Donnelly said, 'We first saw Susan up in Glasgow, she kind of wasn't really chatting to anybody just sitting alone in a corner. So we didn't really take that much notice of her. We kind of sent her on stage and then if I'm honest with you our thoughts turned to what we were going to have for lunch.'

Anthony McPartlin had a similar memory. 'We

thought, "Ah here we go, another one of those. We've got another one of those." Susan was nervous, she was definitely nervous.'

During the show, in which Morgan presented Susan with a triple platinum record for selling over a million copies of her album, Simon Cowell also discussed his feelings that day. 'I could actually feel the audience behind me, beginning to get restless, you feel it. They smelled blood, seriously. Within about five seconds of her singing I felt this unbelievable change.

'That was the moment where I thought if she can hit the chorus, this song is going to change her life forever. I could feel it. What I felt during and after the song I don't think I've ever felt at any audition in my life. There was something magical about that audition.'

Talking about her semi-final appearance, with its faltering start, he said, 'She couldn't quite get the top of the song right and for any singer, particularly somebody like her without any experience of live shows, it throws you. Then the first crack appeared. I asked to see her before the final went out. I just cleared the dressing room and said, "I want to talk to you Susan. You don't have to do this." She said, "Simon I've lived all my life on my own, I've dreamed all my life about being a singer this is the one shot and I want to do this." I said, "You're the red hot favourite, which for me means there is a chance you may not win. How are you going to deal with that?" She said, "I still want to enter."'

And when Diversity were announced as the winner? 'Normally I'd look at the winners, this time I'm looking over to my right and I saw a glimmer of fear there: "no one's gonna want me anymore." This was the lowest point we'd ever reached. Where suddenly you go we have a responsibility here, and that's the point where you question yourself, the show and "have we ruined this person's life?"' he said.

'After that tension, however, there had been the triumph of America and the album sales. It's a great human story. Without any hype or without any tricks it's all about her.

'Was Susan Boyle right to dream a dream? Yes. Susan Boyle was good for all of us. She was certainly good for me because I look at me in that first audition and I saw something I didn't particularly like, which was incredibly judgmental. So I think Susan is going to help an awful lot of people who didn't have the confidence to do this.'

A friend of Susan's since childhood, Lorraine Campbell, who had come to London to help Susan cope in those frantic days before the final, also spoke on the programme. Ms Campbell – who said that when she was young Susan had been 'a beautiful looking girl who had beautiful black curly hair… always the classy one' – also helped explain why it all temporarily became too much for Susan.

'She couldn't cope with the paparazzi, that was her biggest problem. She couldn't cope with motorbikes chasing her, journalists undercover in her hotel. These were the pressures that Susan was put under.'

Perhaps Ant summed up the entire phenomenon when he said: 'Where you live, look like, where you're from, it can still happen for you if you believe and you've got the talent.'

And boy, was it 'happening' for Susan by this time. Barely a day went by without an update on her record sales around the world and such was the mania for news about her that the hugely popular *Sun* even devoted a large article to her front door, a white mock-Georgian affair, and how it had become one of the most famous doors in the world!

By the end of the first week in December the album had sold 3.3 million copies worldwide and she had reportedly earned as much in two weeks as previous winner Paul Potts had made in two years, an estimated £5 million. She decided to spend some of that money – by buying a new fridge and a burgundy leather three-piece suite for her home in Blackburn.

On the day of transmission of the Piers Morgan-hosted show the album was still top of the charts in both Britain and America, although she had to call off a planned visit to Canada to appear at Toronto's Waterfall Stage on 21 December. 'Unfortunately Susan will no longer be visiting Canada at the end of this year. The trip will be rescheduled for 2010 to allow more time between international promotional trips,' a spokesman said.

The artist she had replaced at the top of the charts in America could hardly have been more different from Susan. Lady Gaga, the exotic singer/performance artist, was a musical, and physical, universe away from Susan. Her album 'The Fame Monster' was pushed from the top slot in the States by Susan but she said, 'I love Susan Boyle, she is my woman of the year – I don't know if we could work together, but never say never. Our styles are different. It would be great to work with somebody of that talent. She has achieved more in this year than most artists will in a lifetime. This time last year nobody even knew who she was and now she is knocking the world's most established artists off the album and singles charts. I have watched the clip of her singing on *BGT* a thousand times and every time I see Simon Cowell's face, it makes me laugh out loud. He thinks he knows everything but even he wasn't expecting that.'

On 15 December came a double-whammy: two announcements that showed the impact she had made. YouTube announced its most watched videos for the first time since its 2005 inception – and Susan's *BGT* appearance was put into its true, and astonishing, perspective. It had attracted 120 million views around the world, more than the next three most-watched put together.

The second spot, with more than 37 million views, was held by 'David After Dentist', which featured a 7-year-old boy recovering from some dental work that left him feeling disoriented and wondering if he would ever feel normal again.

Third place, with 33 million views, went to 'JK Wedding Entrance Dance', which captured an elaborate routine orchestrated by Jill Peterson and Kevin Heinz – flanked by their bridesmaids and groomsmen – just before their marriage.

A movie trailer for *The Twilight Saga: New Moon* attracted 31 million views, helped by co-stars Robert Pattinson and Taylor Lautner, who had teenage girls swooning over them. But none of them could approach Susan's popularity.

And there was massive news about her album *I Dreamed A Dream*, which was produced by Steve Mac, who had worked with a host of hit artists including Westlife, Ronan Keating and Charlotte Church. By the end of the year Susan had easily won top spot as album of the year in the UK with sales of more than 1.5 million copies in six weeks. It was a similar story in America where she was No. 1 on the *Billboard* album chart for a fifth consecutive week, notching up another 510,000 sales and making her the first artist in the 53-year history of the chart to have a debut album open No. 1 and stay in that position for the following four weeks. As the year drew to an end Susan had sold a total of 2,982,000 albums Stateside.

Australia, too, had succumbed to her appeal. In Christmas week she sold more copies of *I Dreamed A*

Dream than the other top five albums combined. She became the first artist in the country to sell over 100,000 copies for two consecutive weeks, and totalled 450,000 for the five weeks since it had been released.

It was the same story in the *Billboard* 'Pan-European' charts, which showed it was the largest-selling album across the continent.

The rest of the world wasn't immune either. Screaming fans, many of them clutching bouquets of flowers in welcome, greeted her when she landed at Tokyo airport to record a New Year's Eve music special for Japanese television. Two men in the crowd even proposed to her.

'There is so much affection for Susan. She is an idol to us, everyone wants to meet her,' said fan Akiyama Hanako, 56, who had waited seven hours to see her. 'I was near the front but got pushed aside when she appeared. One gentleman kept asking her to marry him over and over again. We have not seen scenes like it since the Beatles.'

In the midst of the travelling, Susan at least managed to spend the Christmas holidays back home in Blackburn. She who had been so eloquent about her torment as a youngster in the classroom, nevertheless found time during her spell back in snowy Scotland to visit two local schools. Bad weather prevented her from attending the cancelled nativity play at the Holy Family Primary School in Winchburgh, but she was determined not to let the children down so she went to their

Christmas party instead and danced with some of the excited youngsters and chatted to them about her music and about the school.

She also visited St. Kentigern's Academy, where she had studied, when a £19-million extension and refurbishment was unveiled. Smartly dressed Susan, wearing a double-breasted military-style coat with gold buttons and a patterned dress, was given a tour of the new facilities and spoke to the staff and children. How strange to think that the woman who had been so troubled in her own childhood was now a VIP in the classroom. No wonder she proclaimed she was the happiest she'd ever been.

'Christmas is a joyous time and this year I'll be with my family and close friends and attending midnight mass to remember the true meaning,' she said. 'It will be a quiet time for reflection. I have so many cards my lounge is full of them and I can barely get in the door. Every one is so special and I've re-read them time and time again.

'The album being so well received is humbling and I'm so very grateful. I hope that everyone is enjoying it.

'It's been an absolutely brilliant year and I can't thank everyone enough for the support I've been given, not only here but around the world. I am the happiest I have ever been and truly enjoying myself. It's been quite a year.'

Susan added, 'God has been very important to me.'

Christmas Day was spent at her sister Bridie's in Motherwell with other members of the family including brothers John, 60, and James, 58, with Susan helping out in the kitchen. After unwrapping a present of slippers and a housecoat from 67-year-old Bridie, Susan put her album on, although she was too modest to sing along with it, and the family then tucked into a meal of vegetable soup, roast beef and trifle.

Even as her official website launched a 'Susan Boyle Store' – items for sale included T-shirts, a tote-bag and a hoodie all adorned with her image or the phrase 'I Dreamed A Dream' – Susan was reflecting on what gave her pleasure in her new life. Not surprisingly, it seemed much of it was the same as it had been before she climbed on board those six buses in the middle of a Scottish January to head towards the *BGT* audition.

Her favourite food was still fish and chips. She still practised singing most days, although she was now careful to rest her voice. She still listened to Michael Bublé, Elton John or 'anybody who can make a really good record.' And her 'very, very favourite' record was still 'Puppy Love' by Donny Osmond.

What will happen to Susan in the years to come? Only time will tell. The initial impact of that Glasgow audition and the YouTube frenzy it ignited must, inevitably, fade. What will not diminish – hopefully not for many years at least – will be the quality of that voice; as clear, light and joyous as a beautiful spring morning in Scotland, yet mature and knowledgeable in a way only years of living a real life can account for. Nor will there be any diminution of the sheer happiness and pleasure she has given and will, no doubt, continue to give. But perhaps Susan's own words about what might happen in the future and her thoughts for those who have come to know and love her, sum it up best:

'Have I found, reached or achieved my dream? Well everybody never completely fulfills their dream. My dream is to make people happy and to go on making people happy for as long at it lasts, so it's not really complete. It's never complete without the fans.'